Happily Ever After

Happily Ever After

MAKING THE TRANSITION
FROM GETTING MARRIED
TO BEING MARRIED

Betsy S. Stone, Ph. D.

DOUBLEDAY
New York London Toronto Sydney Auckland

PUBLISHED BY DOUBLEDAY
a division of Bantam Doubleday Dell Publishing Group, Inc.
1540 Broadway, New York, New York 10036

DOUBLEDAY and the portrayal of an anchor with a dolphin are trademarks
of Doubleday, a division of Bantam Doubleday Dell Publishing Group, Inc.

In order to ensure their privacy, and the confidentiality of the
therapeutic relationship, I have changed the names and
identifying characteristics of my clients.

Book design by Beverley Vawter Gallegos

Library of Congress Cataloging-in-Publication Data
Stone, Betsy S.
Happily ever after: making the transition from getting married to
being married / Betsy S. Stone. — 1st ed.
p.   cm.
1. Marriage—Handbooks, manuals, etc.   I. Title.
HQ734.S8854   1997   96-26133
306.81—dc20   CIP

ISBN 0-385-48316-3
Copyright © 1997 by Betsy S. Stone
All Rights Reserved
Printed in the United States of America
February 1997
First Edition

1   3   5   7   9   10   8   6   4   2

This book is lovingly dedicated
to the man I share my journey with—

my husband, Michael.

THERE ARE SO MANY PEOPLE TO THANK,

so many who helped. Renée, whose idea it was. Pam, who always believes in me, no matter what. Pamela, who pushed me out on my own. Tony, who made it possible. Thanks, I think. Mike, Norma, Don, Mom, Dad, and Grandma, who read and critiqued. Beverly, who listened, even when other stuff was more important. My agent, Jean Naggar, who was patient and supportive. My editor, Frances Jones, whose suggestions were clear and helpful. My patients, who are my best teachers. Thank you for sharing your lives with me. I am grateful for your trust. And, as always, my children, Deborah, Sarah, and Daniel, who keep me understanding how important the future is. I love you.

CONTENTS

CONTENTS

CONTENTS

Happily Ever After

1

HOPES AND DREAMS

JOAN AND CHARLIE FLYNN SAT IN MY PSYCHOTHERAPY office, their tanned hands clasped together. The Flynns were newlyweds, a couple who had been in premarital counseling for four months, as they tried to find ways to communicate with each other. They had entered therapy to work on their relationship, a passionate union that was marked by explosive fighting and long, divisive silences. Joan and Charlie knew that their inability to talk about the difficult aspects of their relationship was undermining their connection to each other, but they could not break through their deadlock of rage and resentment. Their love was strong and evident, but they had to struggle to find common ground in their communication. The wedding itself was a triumph of sorts—for each of them individually, for the two of them as a couple, and for me, their psychologist. We were all proud of ourselves for what they had achieved, though our therapeutic task was far from complete.

Joan was a petite, vivacious speech therapist. She wound her blond, curly hair around her fingers repetitively as she described their wedding and honeymoon. "We didn't even fight with my father," she reported happily. Charlie nodded, with a huge grin. "Although he gave us plenty of opportunities," he added. Both smiled. Charlie was an imposing man, large in both height and build. I always imagined him in his profession of sports trainer, prodding and inspiring his clients to bigger muscles, better endurance, trimmer shape. These were the techniques he had tried to use with his small but determined new wife. Joan continued, "But the funniest part of our wedding week was on the airplane. I cried from LA to Honolulu. Not hard crying, just tears streaming. I felt so bad for Charlie—I looked like a bride sold into marriage against her will." We all smiled, remembering Joan's fears of marriage, her concerns that she would feel trapped. It seemed that her fears had haunted her on the flight. She said, "And then the stewardess came over and asked how long we'd been married. When we said two days, she smiled. It seems that *all* brides cry on the way to Honolulu! What a relief!" Charlie grinned and said, "If you think Joan was relieved, think about me! I was so scared by her fears all last year, and her tears were awful. Thank God it's normal!"

The newlyweds, pleased with the triumph of their wedding and management of the crises they had expected as a part of the marriage ceremony, were unprepared for Joan's intense reaction to *being* married. They thought the wedding would be the end of the road, and that they would now live happily ever after. Even this couple, with four months of productive therapy under their belts, and with at least the verbalized knowledge that "marriage takes work," were deceived by the expectation that they were in the home stretch, that the wedding ceremony would solidify the relationship. Their disappointment at Joan's reaction was camouflaged with amusement at the story, but it was still there.

This couple was not alone in their hopeful expectations of marriage. In some sense, optimism is a *requirement* of early marriage. This all-important conjugal journey cannot be embarked on without the belief that marriage works, that each of us will have our needs met, that love will triumph. Most of us as we enter marriage are even more naïve than the Flynns, without the benefit of premarital counseling. Most of us have no idea what we're getting into when we say "I do." For, although optimism is a necessary ingredient for marriage, it is not enough to sustain a couple through all of the changes that marriage brings.

In addition, it is almost impossible to avoid doom and gloom about marriage and marital success. Statistics on divorce are splashed all over the newspapers and magazines; the numbers are frightening and dismaying. We know that 50 percent of marriages end in divorce. Many of these relationships, fully 32 percent, dissolve before they truly begin, during the "honeymoon" phase of up to 48 months.

What happens in the early years that is so difficult for marriages to endure and survive? A great deal. Couples live together, learn how to stand up for themselves as individuals within the marriage, figure out what a "we" is, deal with extended families, abandon old habits and develop new rituals, negotiate about whose work is more important, see each other in new roles, and try to communicate in productive ways. They figure out how to fill their very different needs for sexuality, intimacy, and social contact, how to be close and how to be separate, how to fight and how to be reconciled. These are enormously difficult tasks, tasks that most people believe can and will be accomplished by love alone.

While Joan and Charlie Flynn—and, indeed, all the couples in this book—are therapy clients from my psychology practice, the issues they faced are faced by all couples in the first years of marriage. Therapy clients are not usually all that different from the rest of the population. They have just chosen to avail themselves of the aid of professionals in their search for marital comfort. Their problems are universal problems; their solutions are common solutions.

Cultural Expectations: The Cinderella Syndrome

One of the most important problems faced by newlyweds is that of cultural expectations. We are all raised on the wonderful myth of marrying and living "happily ever after." The myth, appealing as it may be, often causes a great deal of initial confusion. No one lives happily ever after. Imagine the culture clash faced by Cinderella and Prince Charming. He's used to servants and fine clothes; she's used to being a servant, dressed in rags. He lives in a world of courtiers and parties; her best friends are mice. They have major in-law problems, especially on her side. Are we to believe that these two can surmount their differences easily and simply?

The myths and fairy tales are not mere entertainment; they profoundly influence our perceptions of our relationships. People raised on tales of "happily ever after" expect that outcome in their own relationships. Our imagery of marriage comes from many places in our culture, from fairy tales and books to movies. Adults have icons of marriage and close family life that range from *Married . . . With Children* to *Full House* to the newly liberated Blondie and Dagwood Bumstead. Children derive these images from television shows, books, and movies, such as *Little House on the Prairie* and *Mary Poppins.* And, of course, we are all profoundly influenced by the marriage of our parents. The family each of us was raised in—the family of origin, in psychological jargon—shapes our beliefs about marriage, both in terms of what we expect all marriages to be (our parents') and what we studiously hope to overcome.

Charlie and Joan knew about many of the marital expectations that came from their families of origin. Charlie's parents had what he considered a sterile marriage. He described his parents' relationship in a totally unfavorable light. "They never kissed, never hugged. They barely spoke to each other, not because they were avoiding each other, but because they had nothing to say. I can't imagine my mother telling my father what she did during the day, much less her innermost thoughts. They were simply indifferent to each other. All their passion was reserved for us, the children. They loved us intensely, punished us passionately, taught us as though their lives depended on it."

Joan's parents, by contrast, were enthusiastically involved with each other. They fought and loved at a high-decibel level. Joan couldn't remember a simple discussion between her parents. She did remember being scared by their fighting—and their loving—throughout her childhood.

This juxtaposition of contrasting scenarios is familiar to most therapists. People often seek a mate whose family seems to be the total opposite of their own. Joan and Charlie came into therapy before their marriage in order to stop their pattern of intense quarreling, which was demoralizing for them both. They didn't fight too frequently, but the fighting was extremely painful for both of them. As their psychologist, I could surmise that this had been an area of conflict for both of them before they entered their relationship and that, in fact, they had picked each other because they were unconsciously aware of their differences in this all-important area.

The Issue Is Safety

This part of choosing a mate is a mysterious process. We all look for familiar patterns in our partner—a mate who reminds us of other loved ones in important ways. "She's just like my Mom" is a common reason for a man to give for loving a woman. At the same time (usually not consciously), we pick partners who are struggling with the same issues we confront. Joan and Charlie both grew up in families where there was a lot of emotional "noise," often overwhelming. Joan's family was passionate and loud; Charlie's family was detached and demanding. The two were frightened by the level of emotion in their original families; neither one of them felt safe or loved. In fact, both hoped that their relationship would make them feel more secure. So Joan picked Charlie, at least in part, because he didn't fight and yell. She wanted a husband who wouldn't frighten her with rage and intensity. Charlie picked Joan, at least in part, because she was so passionate. He wanted a marriage in which the central relationship, with all its emotional intensity, lay within the couple and was not beamed toward the children.

Actually, such differences are often what bring people into therapy. That which attracts us to our partner initially may be what we ultimately want to change in the spouse. Joan's passion began to overwhelm Charlie, and his calm demeanor began to feel sterile to her. His prodding and pushing, an approach that was useful in his work, enraged her. Her rage overwhelmed him, and he withdrew. The silences frightened both of them, as neither had ever experienced anything like these awful days without speech.

Often, we choose people whose experiences are different from our own; we are fascinated by their dissimilar skills and hope that their experiences will change us. The wish that marriage will change us is common, though usually unspoken. Marriage will make us happier, more secure, less frantic.

Marriage will repair other losses, such as those caused by previous relationships. Marriage will make us feel lovable, fill the holes inside us. Most of us, if we are honest with ourselves, remember and recognize these hopes—hopes that we will be repaired, cleansed, improved by the simple act of saying "I do." Of course, marriage can be part of some of these changes—a healing environment where personal change is allowed to take place. In fact, this is basic to a healthy marriage. In a good marriage, each person can use the relationship as a safe haven in which to change and grow, accepting the attendant pain of change and growth. Safety, however, is not guaranteed by the wedding, despite our hopes and dreams.

Cinderella hopes that marriage to her prince will allow her to escape from both the drudgery of her former life and the marks it has left. But history always affects our perceptions. How will she react as her marriage and her future unfold? What will she experience when other "Cinderellas" wait on her? What impact has her father's death had? How will she feel when she is relegated to a support role as the prince's status rises? These questions are significant, but they are left unanswered by "happily ever after." How do we each find contentment with our marriage, with its necessary compromises, pleasures, and disappointments? Who teaches us the lessons of marriage, of expectations and losses, of happiness and satisfaction?

Our expectations of marriage are usually mysterious. As with art, we are not sure what we are looking for, but we respond to what we like and dislike. Even though we are not able to articulate what we think should happen, we know when our expectations are *not* met. We expect marriage to change our relationship—and each individual in that relationship. Some of us hope that all our insecurities will be swept away, that a wedding will somehow wash off the pains and disappointment of our emotional lives. Charlie hoped that Joan's trepidation about marriage would dissipate after the wedding, that she would be comfortable with him and their new legal commit-

...ment. He hoped that her emotional intensity would subside. Joan hoped that Charlie would be more emotionally available, less withdrawn at the threat of conflict. We all hope for simple changes—that our spouse will be neater or will swear less. We hope for complicated changes—that marriage will make us better able to understand our own feelings, that we will be more securely loved. And, at times, we hope for unreasonable, impossible changes—that the act of marrying will make us love an unloved fiancée, that legal commitment will bring feelings of belonging and safety, which we have not yet felt.

In this book, you will meet many couples who tried to understand their expectations of marriage and their spouse, couples who successfully negotiated the first years of marriage and became truly "married." You will learn about intimacy and fighting, about relations with in-laws, about the creation of marital rituals. You will learn about the changes that marriage may bring to a relationship, and about finding long-term contentment. You will have an opportunity to explore your own expectations of marriage and those of your mate, and to evaluate how reasonable such expectations are.

In these pages, you will find exercises to illustrate, develop, and refine the skills discussed. Some of the exercises may be easy for you; others may be more difficult. Try all of them, however, because they build upon one another. As you might suppose, some exercises will seem strange and gimmicky to you. Try them anyway—and have fun with them! As you will see, the ability to relax and laugh at yourself will ease many of the transitions of early marriage.

EXERCISE 1: Take out your wedding album and look at the photographs of yourselves and your families. Describe your parents' marriage. Was it happy? Loving? Angry? Distant? How did you hope your marriage would differ from theirs? How did you hope it would be the same as theirs? Then discuss your answers with your partner. Which of your hopes were the same? Which were different?

The Land of Hope

Therapists often hear couples expressing their most powerful and most unrealistic hope—that the spouse will suddenly, easily, and readily understand their innermost feelings. This hope usually includes the wish that our mate will understand us without our having to articulate our feelings. We hope that marriage will give us a place to fulfill that most unattainable, elusive dream—that our loved ones "know" how we feel even before we do ourselves. The yearning for magical understanding is common to most couples in early marriage and may create problems of its own.

Why is understanding our expectations and articulating our hopes so important? Simply put, our expectations are based on our history and the way we have interpreted it. Because humans are creatures of habit, we expect our lives to follow the paths set out for us according to what we "know." Usually, however, we do not know our inner expectations, because they are not conscious. So we expect our lives to follow a pattern without our even knowing, much less saying, what the pattern is. And, given that our expectations are not fully evident to ourselves, imagine how opaque they must be to our new partners.

The inner patterns are usually set in our original families. We learn, at a deep and unconscious level, the behaviors expected of us simply by being in a family and seeing what happens there. We may learn, for example, that men take out the trash and that women care for children and we don't question these "facts" unless someone else follows a different pattern. The simple acceptance of unquestioned information explains why women who have seen their mothers beaten by their fathers do not leave their own physically abusive husbands; they believe, they *know,* that all men beat their wives. Even when they are intellectually aware that other men are not abusive, their experience of abuse makes sense to them, and they remain in potentially lethal marriages. Another woman would leave an abusive man immediately; her expectation is different, so her evaluation of what constitutes appropriate marital behavior is different.

This point illustrates the immense power of expectation. Our expectations are, quite simply, part of our internal blueprint for making a wide variety of evaluations. We anticipate that certain things will happen, and we have emotional reactions when they do not happen. And vice versa. We may be happy or sad, pleased or disappointed, but any variation from the expected will lead to an emotional reaction. I believe that we are almost always thrown off balance—in some sense, even disappointed—when these variations occur, even if we recognize them as changes for the better!

Our disappointment has a simple cause. It requires emotional work to change our evaluation of behavior, to alter our internal blueprint. People may recognize that a different way of behaving might be better for them, but none of us enjoys the changing—until we have incorporated the change into a modified blueprint and begun to enjoy the rewards of being in a different kind of relationship.

EXERCISE 2: Remember dinnertime behavior in your original family. What time did you eat? Who decided what was for dinner? Who cooked it? Where did people sit? Did everyone sit, or did one person serve and hover? Was everyone there, or were certain people absent? Did you have a regular seat at the table, or did you sit wherever you wanted? Did everyone eat the same food? How long did you sit? What did you talk about? Did one person direct the conversation, or did everyone talk?

Was this a full meal or a snack? Was the TV on? Did people wait to be excused from the table, or did they get up when they wanted to? Were there parts of the meal that were unchanging—like bread on the table or milk in the glass? Who cleared the table? Who did the dishes?

These questions, seemingly unimportant, demonstrate the pattern of dinner behavior in your original family. They are far from inclusive, but they begin to describe what you expect at dinnertime—even if you didn't like the way dinners were conducted. To change your expectations requires that you first know your expectations, then evaluate which ones you wish to continue and which you would choose to replace with other behaviors. And becoming aware of our expectations often is the most difficult part.

Our expectations come not only from our society and from our families, but from our fantasies as well. The societal mythology that marriage is a panacea for the problems inherent in all relationships can be destructive to a newlywed couple, because evaluating their relationship against such high standards is difficult. If our hope is for "happily ever after," we are bound to be disappointed. Disappointed hopes, in turn, may lead to a re-evaluation of the relationship and undermine a couple's sense of commitment to each other. When a couple expects marriage to heal all wounds, then reality will feel like a failure. If, on the other hand, the couple has more realistic expectations, reality will seem more reasonable, more workable, more pleasurable.

The hope that simply getting married will have an immediate, permanent effect on a relationship can be equally unrealistic. One couple I worked with, Tom Kelly and Sally Macmillan, had dated and lived together for seven years. For five of those years, Tom had been trying to convince Sally to marry him. She refused until he began to question her commitment to him. She was very clear that she wished to remain in the relationship and that she saw her life with him continuing, but she was not interested in getting married. They came to my office to discuss the unresolvable problem.

Tom was a slight, dark man. His whole body arched forward as he gave an opening "speech." I could tell that he had prepared his remarks, which came out in stilted fashion and, frankly, seemed a little overpowering. He described his many attempts to convince Sally that marriage was good, that it would work, that he loved her. She sat back, silent, sinking into her half of the couch, unable to utter a word through his long presentation. When he finally gave up, exhausted and frustrated, she began to speak. "I can't explain my position, even to myself," she said in a quiet, sad voice. "I love Tom, and I want him to be happy more than anything in the world." Her voice shook with emotion. "He's my friend, and my hopes for the future all involve him. I'm not leaving him, not now, not ever. So why can't I do this thing he so wants? What's crazy is that I'd rather that we have a baby together than get married." She described the house they had purchased and her feeling of commitment to Tom.

"What happens to you when you imagine getting married?" I asked softly. I expected her to talk about her parents' bad marriage, a past experience in a committed relationship, or some very real hurt she had witnessed or experienced. So I was surprised when she simply giggled and said, "Sadie, Sadie, married lady." What did she mean?

Sally looked sheepish and said that she was worried that *she* would change if they got married, and only in negative ways. She thought that she might become more dependent on Tom, that she would see herself only in relation to him. "I don't want to be a *wife*," she said. Somehow the word had powerfully negative connotations for her, implying only dependence and incompetence. She was not going to be a married lady!

Sally's expectations of the wedded state had a profound influence on the relationship between this committed pair. She believed that marriage reduced a woman to a subordinate role, and Tom's assurances could not alter her belief. Our therapeutic work together was helpful in tracing the roots of her conviction, evaluating it, and ultimately changing it. This couple had to learn to deal in an appropriate way with her expectations of marriage and marital change so that they could move on in their relationship.

In many ways, we all expect marriage to change us. Some, like Sally, are at least aware of our deeply held expectations, but most of us are not. Most of us sail into marriage with unspoken hopes and dreams about the effect that marriage will have on us, and most of us are sorely disappointed when these hopes are not fulfilled.

We are usually clearer, though equally naïve, in our expectations about how marriage will change the spouse. Therapists' offices are filled with couples who expected a dramatic change in their spouse after the wedding. He will watch less football; she will be more secure in the relationship; alcohol abuse will stop; she will be less moody; he will stop ogling other women—these and many more hopes are dashed during the honeymoon and new marriage.

The hope that marriage will change our mates is an almost universal one—and it is usually disappointed. In fact, the person we marry is the same person the next day—unchanged by the circumstance of a wedding. Even though this seems to be intellectually obvious to us, the expectation is so widely shared that it is hard to avoid. There is nothing essentially transformative about a marriage. We stand in front of a community and make promises, but we are not dramatically altered by this act. Our joy in the relationship exists just as it did the day before the wedding—and so do our discomforts. Problems and disturbances in relationships outlast the wedding night; but ideally, so will our delight and happiness.

SUGGESTIONS FOR FURTHER THOUGHT

- Make a list of your hopes and dreams. Remember: there are no right or wrong answers. Also, although these can include material things—children, a house—they should also include hopes for your relationship—we'll learn how to fight, we'll always be passionate, etc.

- Expectations are different from hopes—they reflect our ideals and demonstrate the reality we anticipate. Do you expect your spouse to hurt or support you? Do you expect your spouse to make you happy, to allow you to be happy, to get in the way of your happiness?

- Talk about where the hopes may come from, and the emotions each of you feel about them.

- Talk about where you and your spouse agree and disagree—and why.

Cinderella and her prince marry
and settle down to live their lives together in
the palace. Does she continue to treat him like a prince,
or is he simply her husband? What's the difference?
Does she curtsey to her husband? What is her role in his
life? In the kingdom? What is his role in her life? How do
they learn to make joint decisions?

2

MARITAL RULES VS. SOCIAL RULES

LL RELATIONSHIPS ARE DRIVEN BY SPOKEN
and unspoken rules of behavior; these guidelines tell us
how we are expected to act. This is an "outline" of
acceptability that exists in different forms in every
relationship. We know how to speak with our bosses and our
best friends. We have certain expectations for interactions with
our employees, our children, and the person at the grocery
check-out counter. But we are generally unaware of these
regulations unless they are broken. Then we are surprised at, and
occasionally offended by, the insensitivity of the other person.

These rules are always present in our interactions and are
often most noticeable in our patterns of communication. We

speak differently to different people. I am much more likely to swear, for example, with my friends and spouse than with my children or strangers. The tone of my voice changes when I talk with my husband or my patients. I speak to a phone salesperson differently from the way I speak to my friends. My children can often identify *who* I am talking to on the phone simply by listening to *how* I am talking.

Mary Jo and Larry Miller came into therapy after two years of a bitter, angry marriage. They had lived together before exchanging vows, but each expected the marriage ceremony to have a significant effect on their relationship, to solve their problems. They had a litany of complaints about each other, ranging from involvement with the family of origin to the cleanliness of the home to Mary Jo's work hours. Trying to have them recall happier times, I asked what had brought them together originally, what had attracted them to each other. Their answers surprised even them, and were an indication to me of how much work needed to be done.

Mary Jo, a tall blond woman who worked the night shift in a large urban hospital emergency room, described Larry as a needy and demanding man, who believed she was responsible for taking care of him and for being there whenever he was home. He wanted, according to her, his dinner on the table and his wife admiring him. She, on the other hand, wanted to be a good nurse, to work her demanding shift, and to come home to someone who would accept her for what she could offer and not notice only what she didn't offer.

Larry was squirming in his chair; I wondered whether he wanted to talk or to get away. Noting that Mary Jo had not answered my question, I put the same question to him.

"Oh, I thought she would save me," he answered. His words were striking, coming from this burly truck driver. He was obviously capable of taking care of himself—certainly in a fight. He had described being on the road for at least twenty days per month, living competently on his own.

"Save you?" I repeated as a question.

"Sure. Get me away from my parents, teach me to have friends, have fun with me."

A tall order, I thought. Suddenly, this angry couple seemed like two little kids, each seeing the other as the answer to unspoken needs. Mary Jo wanted approval and a safe place to relax; Larry wanted someone who would challenge him to change. I asked how she had done at filling his tall order.

"Lousy. She's stopped doing it—and that's when I realized that she doesn't love me enough." He looked at her, a look that was half-glare and half-request. Mary Jo's response was automatic. She seemed to have heard all this before, and knew what he expected to hear. "Of course I love you. I just hate how much you need me. And you need me so much more since we got married. I can't go out with friends; I have to be there for you all the time—even though you're not there for me lots of the time!" Mary Jo had adapted to the distance Larry's work imposed on their relationship. In fact, she reveled in it. She loved her privacy, her independence. But she could not tell him how she felt—because he could not bear to hear it.

The Millers were responding to each other automatically. Larry's request for reassurance brought her to say that she loved him, but that did not make him feel loved. Mary Jo's rebuff of his demands made him come closer to her, but did not provide her with the privacy and approval she wanted. Small wonder they were so frustrated. Neither was getting what he or she wanted, and both were pursuing the other in fruitless ways.

Figuring Out the Rules

We all expect that marriage changes *people*. I believe, however, that marriage changes the rules. Each of us goes through life following many rules, most of them unspoken. We do not punch our boss when he or she demands that we stay late one more time or takes credit for our work; we generally obey the law; we eat breakfast foods in the morning instead of spaghetti at 7 A.M. (even if we prefer spaghetti). Some of the rules are so taken for granted that we have no need to speak of them; others need constant mention. Many rules are followed because they have specific consequences, known either explicitly or implicitly. Kids do their homework to get good grades and win their parents' approval; people wash dishes so that there will be clean dishes to eat on later; we return phone calls from other people. We follow these rules because we want to avoid feeling guilty or because obedience makes us feel better about ourselves, and we obey societal strictures to gain rewards—like good grades or a raise or a smile. We follow them to gain the favor of others and to experience ourselves in a good light. And we follow the rules to avoid being caught not following them. For example, many of us drive more slowly when we see a police car. We may all agree that speed limits are important, but we are more likely to obey them when an infraction brings the danger of a response.

It is essential for any society or group of people to have rules. Without them, we would be unable to coexist, randomly following whatever desires we may have at the moment. But sometimes rules confuse us, and sometimes they are downright destructive, such as the rules that limit the behavioral options of people based solely on their race, gender, or social class.

In marriage our perception of acceptable behaviors changes. Rules about politeness and kindness are often abandoned during a fight; rules about intimacy are trampled on in a crisis. We behave in ways we find uncomfortable, and we see our spouse do things we think are wrong, rude, or simply bad. Relationships change when you see your spouse at his or her worst, and when you realize that you will see this person doing similar things every day for the rest of your life! So if your mate belches every morning on awakening, or doesn't remember to call you when he or she is going to be home late, or forgets your anniversary, you'll look on these behaviors as permanent—and overwhelming—unless you talk about them. Yet talking about them may be perceived as criticizing your mate, and discussing certain subjects may even be embarrassing to both of you.

Ultimately, the rules have to change—to be redefined, negotiated, and refined—if marriage is to work. People who have been in long-term marriages know that the rules are different and that they evolve over time. Spouses can and must tell each other things they tell no one else: you look fat, your breath stinks, I'm scared when you yell. Many of us try out new thoughts with our spouse before we tell anyone else: I want to quit my job, have a baby, I'm afraid I have a lump in my breast. Part of the task of early marriage is negotiating from the rules of social relationships to the rules of *this* marital relationship.

How can people do this? For most of us, it is a process full of confusion and uncertainty. The stakes are enormously high, and the rules of play are not clear. This is the time when patterns of negotiation are laid down. Some couples blossom in the new situation and see each other as a treasured confidant. They are able to communicate enough (but not too much) about their needs and expectations and can respond to the information they receive. Others, like Mary Jo and Larry, are stymied.

The pattern followed by Mary Jo and Larry was much clearer to me than it was to them. In fact, their customary ways of behaving were actually obscuring the possibility of a reasonable solution. Each wanted things from the other and had made some efforts to get what was needed. When their efforts failed, however, they kept trying to get what they wanted in the same way, over and over again. Like children who cannot tolerate the refusal of a treasured toy, this couple kept saying PLEASE at higher and higher intensity, hoping to force the other's hand.

Such an approach rarely works in the long run. Although Larry was able to get Mary Jo to say she loved him, he still felt frustrated. Mary Jo told Larry how debilitating his dependence was, but he didn't change. They were continually startled by the intensity of their rage and fighting, and dismayed by the repetition.

Ambivalence

"I have never hated anyone as much as I hate Larry," Mary Jo explained later. "He makes me feel trapped, as though my feelings are unimportant. But at the same time, I want to tell him things, to share my day with him." This dichotomy of love and hate surprises many couples in early marriage—that it's there at all, and that it's so intense. Larry couldn't understand Mary Jo's feelings of being trapped, because he experienced marriage as the "safest place I've ever been." His commitment to Mary Jo was a psychological home base, a refuge from the hardships in his life. He knew he could take care of himself as long as she was there when he wanted her, rather like a lamp that can be turned on when needed. But this was the last thing Mary Jo wanted to be!

The dichotomy of liking and disliking, love and hate, rage and need is an absolutely normal part of all intense human relationships, but it surprises most newlyweds. Parents and children feel it throughout their lives together. Most of us even feel the switch between intense positive and negative emotions toward loved ones who have died. It is normal, but it is also frightening, because society's expectations appear to dictate that we love and enjoy our mates, and that we feel good about them all the time. Our "failure" to do so is disappointing and unpleasant, and makes many of us doubt our commitment and our choice. It may change our attitude toward our relationships, making them less a refuge and comfort, more a place of danger and hopelessness.

The Millers certainly thought their problems were hopeless.

What Mary Jo wanted was what Larry most feared. What he wanted was intolerable to her. Both felt that unless they prevailed, they couldn't survive in the marriage, yet if either of them "won," the other would lose everything he or she needed. They felt completely stuck, and furious about the impasse they had reached.

Control

This battle was not only a battle over behavior. By the time I saw the couple, they were no longer fighting about how each should act. They were fighting for control.

EXERCISE 3: Members of each couple have areas they care about to a greater or lesser extent. These decision areas are usually divided according to each person's needs. For example, one person may have a greater need for social contacts, so that person may be in charge of the couple's social calendar. One may need to have tight control over finances. In your relationship, how are decisions made? What areas belong primarily to you and which to your mate? When does each of you have veto power—and how often do you use it? What happens when the veto power is overused?

Each of us has a need for control. Whether we emphasize the areas of privacy or self-expression or sexuality, we need to know that our desires and requirements are being attended to by the important people in our lives. Given this need for power, it is not surprising that we demand more control when we feel least in control.

How does this work? By the time I saw Larry and Mary Jo, their arguments were no longer about how to get what they wanted, but were battles for power. Each felt the other was unresponsive, so each demanded more and more. This spiral was counterproductive and destructive.

Control is an important issue in all close relationships, and is especially so in marriage. We all need to feel important in the world, and controlling others is a sure way to feel that. Early marriage presents us with opportunity after opportunity to battle for control. We can argue about whose parents we spend holidays with, where we hang this picture, who picks up clothing, who does which chores, how we talk to each other, and, of course, where we should squeeze the toothpaste tube and how the toilet paper rolls.

Battles over control are of paramount importance in the emotional development of every couple's relationship. Each of us needs to learn how to fight with our partner. Every couple has to develop rules—both spoken and unspoken—for acceptable behavior in a fight. Some couples yell and scream; others find such behavior intolerable. Some couples carry out quarrels in public or before friends; some discuss their intimate arguments only in private. We all need to learn how and when to lose a battle. Whatever the rules ultimately established by an individual pair, the process of drawing up the rules for marital scrimmages begins early in the relationship, changes during the first few years of marriage, and reasserts itself in each and every marital crisis.

Creating the Rules

This process is counterintuitive for most couples. When we marry, we do not expect to find ourselves in battles with our intimate partners. Instead, we expect our relationships to be peaceful and positive. But the truth is that we have to learn how to fight—and how to fight safely. We must learn what each of us needs to make the fight productive—because fighting *is* productive, if it is done well. And fighting is important. Every couple argues, so every couple needs to know *how* to argue. We will discuss how to fight productively in greater detail in Chapter 8.

How do we learn how to fight? The "rules of engagement" are based on a combination of personal history and present-day negotiation. Couples bring two sets of rules—those of each family of origin—to the table and negotiate from there. Usually, the negotiations are not conscious. We expect behaviors that were acceptable in our parents' marriages to be acceptable in our own. So if women yell at men and men ignore yelling women in our family of origin, we expect women to yell at men and men to ignore women in our own marriage. Negotiation begins if, and only if, each party objects to the partner's expectations. If a husband listens to his yelling wife or objects to being yelled at, or if a wife doesn't yell when she has something to say or expects her words to be attended to, then the couple has to find alternative behaviors that will work for them. The outcome of this negotiation is the new rule.

Mary Jo and Larry had established many poor rules in their marriage. One of the most obvious—and most destructive—was a very common one: that people are required only to talk and to listen in intimate relationships. But words alone do not produce change. Each heard the other describe what was wrong but did nothing to try to improve their interactions; they felt trapped rather than freed by their knowledge of the other's needs.

Mary Jo and Larry had a second, similarly unspoken rule. Again, it is a common one, subscribed to by many couples. They believed it was more intimate to talk about problems than to talk about the pleasurable aspects of their relationship. Each felt comfortable telling the other all the myriad things they disliked about the partner, but they rarely shared what they liked! Each apparently expected that the other one *knew* what was good. In fact, each was worried that the partner didn't like him or her at all, because the other hadn't mentioned in a long time what was likable.

Choosing to Make Good Rules

Establishing good, effective rules is actually much harder than establishing bad ones. We seem to fall into bad rules almost without thinking. In contrast, most couples need to work on developing good rules. But how do we go about doing this?

The first steps are not simple, because they require us to attend to parts of ourselves that we often overlook or aren't even aware of. To begin, we need to examine our responses to various parts of our relationships, to figure out what we like and don't like. This sounds easier than it is. Most of us are blissfully unaware of many of our emotional responses to different situations. We don't quite know why we're feeling happy or sad or anxious. Often, we aren't even aware what it is that we do feel. For example, Larry didn't know that he was lonely on the road, so he couldn't tell Mary Jo about his feelings of isolation. Instead, his response to the loneliness was to be demanding and petulant when he returned. Had he been able to describe his feelings to his wife, she might have responded to his needs. The response would have been a genuine reaction to deep feelings. Instead, she responded guiltily to his secondary feelings of need.

Realistic negotiation requires that we assess our own emotional reactions, because they are our most important tools for understanding.

EXERCISE 4: Imagine that your spouse has done something you really like—made your favorite dinner, brought you flowers, supported you in your work in an important way. How do you feel? Happy? Excited? Are you wondering what he or she expects in return? Do you want to hug or touch your partner? Do you want to tell your partner how you feel, or are you more comfortable showing your feelings in another way? Would your feelings be different if your partner's behavior was an apology for some slight? Would your feelings be different if your partner was helping you celebrate an achievement, or comforting you after a painful hurt? Notice how your feelings and responses change under different circumstances.

The next step is to communicate these reactions to our partners. We need to find a way to tell our mates how we feel, but our communications cannot be made in the heat of anger. In fact, discussion does not happen when we're yelling; we cannot hear things said to us by an angry partner. Although Mary Jo and Larry had some understanding of how the other one felt, they shared their true feelings only in moments of rage and disappointment. One of the initial—and most crucial—aspects of therapy for this couple was that they had a place where they could talk, rather than yell, about their feelings. For most people, yelling guarantees that the other person won't listen to or hear you. Mary Jo and Larry had perfected this form of noncommunication!

How do we communicate our feelings so that they can truly be heard? The simple answer is to talk to our partners about them, but that's easier said than done. Obviously, we must be sensitive to the receptivity of our mates and to our own style of presentation. We must talk about how *we* feel—not about how the *other* person should or does feel. The temptation to explain our partner's feelings rather than our own is common, but it is rarely an effective device. A woman is more likely to try to tell her husband what he feels, at least in part because the language of feelings is one that women are more comfortable with than men. Men may, and frequently do, invite women to take on the task of "talking feelings," because it seems easier to have someone else do your emotional work. I believe this to be a dangerous pattern. It can be insulting to have someone else explain your feelings to you, and, frankly, it's hard to do so accurately. Therapists go to school for years to be able to help people recognize their feelings—and we're not always on target. Marital partners need to learn to do their own emotional work, not try to do each other's.

> EXERCISE 5: Remember your scenario in Exercise 4. Your partner has done something that pleases you. How are you going to communicate your reaction? Use an "I" statement. The format of an "I" statement is simple: I feel _____ (emotion) when you do _____ (action) because it makes me _____ (feeling statement). For example: I feel happy when you bring me flowers, because it makes me feel you thought about me during the day. Or: I am glad that you did the dishes, because I am simply too tired tonight. Or: Thanks for coming to my work dinner. I enjoyed having you there.
>
> Some couples prefer to communicate emotional messages through touch, that is, a hug or a kiss. This is a lovely way to tell your partner that he or she has pleased you, but it's not very specific. You must *also* use words, so that your partner knows exactly what part of his or her behavior you liked.

A third important step toward negotiation of new rules is to listen. Again, this is harder than it sounds. We generally don't like hearing opinions that differ from our own, especially from our life's partner. So Larry could not tolerate hearing how much Mary Jo valued her independence; it was too inconsistent with how he felt. The difference seemed to him to indicate that she did not care about him at all. This is a common mistake. We often misinterpret our partner's different perceptions as an indication that he or she is not as invested or involved in the relationship, rather than that he or she sees the world differently from the way we see it. In many marital relationships, people feel their partners should see the world in the same way, that loving means agreeing. This is a fantasy that can create lots of problems.

Marriages are made of individuals coming together, and individuals do not always think the same thoughts. In solid relationships, one and one do not add up to one; they add up to two separate and individual beings who are connected by their bond.

> EXERCISE 6: Listening is as important a part of communication as finding the right words at the right time. It requires that two people not only say what they mean, but that they also check out what each other has heard. Do this exercise with your partner. It will feel silly at first, but keep trying. Tell your partner something that has emotional importance to you, and ask your partner to repeat it in his or her own words. It is important that your mate does not use your words, but puts your statement into his or her language. Be sure that you understand what he or she is telling you, and that it fits with what you are trying to communicate. The first few times you try this, be sure that you are not being critical of your partner; this will decrease his or her ability to listen. Do the exercise, with you making statements and your partner rephrasing them, for about five minutes— and that's a long time! After you talk and your partner listens and rephrases, reverse positions. Do the exercise for another five minutes. If you do this exercise daily, you will find that your communication improves altogether. UNDERSTAND THAT LISTENING IS NOT AGREEMENT. JUST BECAUSE SOMEONE HEARS YOU DOES NOT GUARANTEE THAT HE OR SHE THINKS YOUR IDEAS ARE CORRECT.

As we learn to understand, communicate, and take responsibility for our authentic feelings and thoughts, we can begin to adapt to our partner's very different needs. For Larry and Mary Jo, this did not turn out to be a long process; we spent a few sessions helping them understand and accept their emotional differences. As Larry became gradually able to hear that Mary Jo enjoyed his time on the road, he could tell her he had always felt guilty—and sad—about leaving her. She reassured him that his time away made their time together more exciting for her—when he was fun to be with! They talked about ways that he could return to their home more positively—talk more often from the road, warn her when he would be back in town, come home and be happy to see her. We also discussed the ways she could welcome him and make him feel important—hug him, tell him stories about what had happened while he was gone, stay at home while he was at home. We focused on what each of them wanted, not on who was to blame for what they currently had. Some of the negotiations got heated, but the couple persevered. We began to meet less and less often, as they did more of their work outside the therapy sessions. Then, one day, I got a frantic phone call from Mary Jo.

"He wants to have a baby!" She sounded terrified and overwhelmed. "Another responsibility for me!" We set up an appointment for later that day, and they walked in, looking angry and sheepish. Angry that they were in another crisis, sheepish that it had become a crisis.

But sitting in my office, a safe place, where they could use all their communication skills, this couple did what they now knew how to do so well: they began to negotiate. They talked about what each of them wanted, and why. They listened to each other, without the powerful pull of intense emotional reactivity. They realized that they would not solve the problem in one hour, in one day, and they gave themselves time to think, feel, listen, and wait. These are the skills that each couple needs to negotiate the rules of their special relationship. Larry and Mary Jo had already learned these skills, and they could now put them to use.

Their skills are skills that all couples need. They are skills that all of us, even after years of successful marriage, need to work on and be aware of. We constantly need to update our ability to know ourselves, to communicate our feelings, to listen, and to talk. Ultimately, Mary Jo and Larry were able to work on their problems with caring communication and constructive change. All of us in relationships must be able to do just that.

SUGGESTIONS FOR FURTHER THOUGHT

- What rules have you brought to your marriage?
- Which of these rules are useful? Which are no longer useful?
- Have you and your partner created new rules within the framework of this relationship? How?
- How can you continue to create and refine new rules when the old ones no longer apply?

Prince Charming expects that
everyone will listen to him; he is, after all, the
Prince of the Realm! But Cinderella isn't used to talking
to other people—she's used to taking orders, not making
her wishes known. What happens when this young couple
tries to communicate? She doesn't know how to be
respected, and he expects too much respect.
How can they talk like equals?

3

COMMUNICATION

JILL AND FRANK CURDY SAT COMFORTABLY IN
my office. I had seen them twice before, dealing with various
topics, none of them difficult to resolve. I was waiting for the
real issues to surface. It is common for couples to try out a
therapist, presenting problems as an opportunity to see the
"expert" in action. I knew that I had passed their tests, and I was
curious. What was going to happen next? When would the meat
of the work begin?

Jill, a slender, anxious woman, was dressed for work. She
appeared matronly, with lace on her floral dress. Her job as an
employment counselor was challenging and well paid. I
imagined that she presented herself as professional and

competent in her workplace, to have progressed as quickly as she had. However, she seemed to me immature and unsure. She looked at Frank for his consent before she began to speak. I followed her gaze. Her husband was a tall, lanky man with bitten fingernails. Frank was in constant motion. His leg jerked spasmodically; his fingers drummed the couch; his teeth chewed his tongue. He seemed impatient, verging on angry. He was less successful than his wife, having hit a "glass ceiling" at his computer software company. He seemed to accept his professional plateau, at least verbally. I wondered how he really felt about supporting his wife's meteoric rise, but did not pursue the question. I waited for them to begin.

Jill looked out the window at the gray November day. It was drizzling and cold. Slowly she began to speak. "I keep asking Frank where he wants to go for Thanksgiving and Christmas. My mother has invited us, but she says that she'll understand if we have to spend one of the holidays with Frank's family. I want to be with my family—I really miss them. So I want to go home for Christmas—it's the longer holiday."

I looked at Frank, expecting a response. He was silent. I waited a few moments and then asked him, "What do you want to do?"

He spoke slowly. "Whatever Jill wants is okay with me." I didn't believe him for a moment. Something about the way he said it, or the way he looked, made it clear that there was more going on here than a discussion about holidays. I asked him, "Is that really true? Do you really want her to decide without your input?"

"Well, if it matters so much to her." He seemed angry, pressured, and wouldn't look at Jill or me. What was going on here? Frank was sending out intense emotional messages, but I was unsure what he was trying to communicate. Jill looked at me, clearly asking for help. Did she know what his signals meant? I needed a translator, but I was not going to ask Jill to do Frank's work for him. So I addressed my next statement to him. "I'm confused. There's more going on here than vacation plans. Can you tell me why this discussion is making you so tight?"

"I'm not tight. Jill can decide. Whatever she says is fine, just fine." His tone of voice belied his words. It was not "fine" to have Jill decide. In fact, whatever Jill chose was likely to begin a quarrel, a distracting quarrel. There was an issue here that needed to be addressed before any discussion could occur.

Because of the many messages being sent, much of the Curdys' communication was confusing. The discrepancy between what Frank was saying and the way he was saying it was vast. He sounded petulant and angry, though his words indicated flexibility and cooperation. Jill appeared dependent and needy, a presentation of self that was inconsistent with the powerful woman I knew her to be, at least in the workplace. What was happening here—and how could I help her regain her strength at the same time as he began to speak honestly for himself?

This pattern of confusing messages is common for married people. It is sad, but true, that we humans often tell each other things we do not mean. Frank was saying he was willing to go along with Jill, to cooperate. But he didn't want to, and the tone of his voice and body language were letting her know that, clearly and unambiguously. To improve their communication, a lot had to change!

Frank had to come to terms with his own feelings and attribute emotional weight to what he wanted. He had to develop the ability to tell Jill what mattered to him, and she had to listen to and consider—though not necessarily give in to—his needs. Jill had to deal with Frank in a respectful, nondependent manner. They had to develop a method of talking and listening to each other so that their communication could go beyond simple arrangements, to the higher plane of emotional exchange. Most important, they had to be able to take the risks entailed in clearer communication.

What Is Communication?

What is true communication? For each person, in each situation, communication is a different experience. There is no way to objectify it. The experience of being understood is, quite simply, totally subjective. Even the subjects of communication are idiosyncratic. For some of us, simple exchanges like "What did you do today?" are intimate and personal. For others, they are informational and impersonal. There is no single right way to communicate. Like beauty, communication is in the eye (and ear) of the beholder.

Because communication is subjective, each person in a relationship must negotiate to get his or her own needs met. Each partner must participate in the development of rules for communication. We do this so often that we are usually unaware of establishing "communication regulations."

Some rules are universal. We speak the shared language of our partner in a verbal exchange—English to English-speakers, French to French-speakers. Remember the brouhaha when Heather Whitestone, the first deaf Miss America, spoke aloud to a group of hearing-impaired adults? They were outraged that she did not use sign language to send her message, even though she is not facile at signing and had a sign interpreter. We expect each other to opt for the easiest shared language.

Some rules are cultural. French people kiss when they meet; most British people do not. Some Italians and Jews talk with their hands, and it may be culturally acceptable for their voices to be raised. Asians generally speak more quietly and bow to show respect.

Some rules are role-specific. We may assume, for example, that men are less capable of explaining their feelings, and that women always know where things are. We may assume that teachers have infinite patience, that lawyers always believe in the innocence of their clients, and that actors are similar to the roles they play.

Some rules—in fact, most rules—are specific to an individual relationship. We do not usually yell at our bosses. Most adolescents do stomp around their homes. We cry in front of certain people and not others. We curse in some situations and not in others. We have specific people we tell specific secrets, and we expect a reliable response.

One of the first tasks of any relationship is finding a common language. While we all expect this to be easy—we generally marry people who speak the primary language we do—it actually is quite difficult. Words have different meanings for each of us. We rarely investigate the intent of other people's words; rather, we expect that everyone means the same thing by the same words. In fact, trying to understand the meanings of other people's words is one of the first tasks of any therapy, whether individual, marital, group, or family therapy.

It is quite common for people to come to therapy complaining, "We don't communicate anymore." My immediate response to this statement is "Tell me what you mean by that. What is communication? What does it feel like when you're communicating?" I find it interesting that, although it is hard to describe what communication is, it is simple to explain what it feels like.

We all know when we've been heard. We feel validated, comfortable, respected. The other person has looked us in the eye and listened. It feels important and right. Simply put, it feels good to communicate.

We also know when we don't feel heard. We feel diminished, ignored. The experience is that of being unimportant, uncared for. It makes us feel hurt, or angry and withdrawn. It feels awful.

While we may know the experience of being heard and respected, as well as that of being ignored, we find it difficult to describe what communication actually is. Bookstores have shelves and shelves of tomes on this difficult topic, books describing gender and racial differences in communication, how-to books outlining effective communication, and many books bemoaning our pitiful failures at this essential task. And yet we persist in our attempts to communicate, because it is a crucial aspect of human interaction. We need to communicate to feel connected. All animals have a need to attach, whether through ranking or touch or some form of auditory exchange. We share this need with other members of the animal world. We need to link, to interact, to know our place in the world and *vis-à-vis* each other. Verbal communication is only a small part of our informational exchange. Many of us are actually clearer in our nonverbal communication, the exchange of information based on history, inference, and interpretation.

Nonverbal Communication

The Curdys were far from able to communicate well, but there was no question in my mind that they were communicating. It is virtually impossible for humans to avoid communication. There is an exchange of information in our silences, our glances, our stares, and our grunts. We attribute meanings to the ways we sit or stand, hold our eyes and heads, use our hands. Before we even look at verbal communication, we must understand the other kinds of nonverbal exchanges we have. It is imperative that we think about all the levels of interpersonal communication, because they all influence our experiences.

EXERCISE 7: *Listen* to one of your favorite television shows without the picture, either by turning the brightness to black, or by turning your back to the TV set. Notice how much less information you receive, and how much you want to turn back toward the set. Try the same exercise with each other: talk without any visual contact. Your communication may feel less complete, more frustrating.

Many of us experience a similar sense of disconnectedness when we speak on the telephone, lacking our familiar visual cues. Hints such as body language and facial expressions help us evaluate the process and content of our interaction with another person. From these visual bytes of information, we assess whether others are telling us the truth, whether they are happy about what they are saying, whether they are even paying attention.

Nonverbal communication is a basic part of our conversational repertoire. There are lots of ways to tell other people what we think, or how we feel, without using words to describe our experience. Examples range from the serious to the ridiculous. It is easy, for instance, to let someone know that you are bored with him. You can look away, pick up the newspaper or a book, walk off, or even fall asleep. It is easy to tell another person that you are interested. You can look at him directly, nod, move closer, smile. All of these reactions affect the other person's experience of the conversation—and his sense of his value to you.

Indirect Communication

We also use words to send "coded" messages. These are communications whose meaning is known to the people involved but is not directly stated. My husband knows, for example, that if I go to take a bath, it means I want to be alone. There is no association between taking a bath and solitude—at least for other people. But Mike and I both know the subliminal message in my words "I'm going to take a bath." My message has nothing to do with cleanliness. It is a statement that I need privacy, time by myself. He may even respond by asking whether I'm OK!

Each of us has similar examples of nonverbal and indirect communication. We look at our partner in a particular way or make a subtle hand signal that means, "I'm ready to go" when we want to leave a social gathering. Another gesture may mean, "I need to get out of here—RIGHT NOW!" We may use a particular word to send the message to stop drinking, or to relax, or to indicate that we cannot remember the name of the person we *should* be introducing. These signals between partners are useful, telling each other what we need and want, and reminding each other of the intimacy we share. In fact, it feels strange to see other couples employing our personal signals! At its best, nonverbal communication sends the implicit message that we know each other well, that we are a unit, that we are, in some important sense, separate from other people and other couples.

At worst, nonverbal or indirect communication is a horrible mess. This complicated process requires the involvement of at least two people—one who tries to get ideas across, and one who interprets the amalgam of speech and silence, voice and body posture, through his own filters. Poorly interpreted signals lead to resentment and confusion. We feel misunderstood, that our needs are being ignored. In the Curdys' case, Frank's words told Jill that he was willing to put aside his own wishes in deference to hers. But his indirect communication was telling her that his words were untrue—that she should not accept his statements at face value. Both forms of communication are equally clear: his avowal of willingness and flexibility as well as his nonverbal denial of his statements were true. They just happened to be mutually exclusive!

This kind of contradictory communication, especially in an otherwise capable couple, is an indication of high tension. Something "hot" was happening. I didn't know whether the issue was the topic being discussed or something else, but I knew it was my job to help them sort out the tangle and defuse the stress. Jill and Frank needed to understand his confusing messages and see what purpose this mess served. For it is usually true that people make messes for a reason.

Why were the Curdys making this mess? I assumed that, at

least for Frank, the contradictory messages served a purpose. He was trying to tell Jill something important, something he could not say directly. His convoluted communication was both a solution to a problem—and a problem in itself.

Most of the "symptoms" couples develop are, in fact, solutions. In this case, Frank had something important to tell Jill, but he felt incapable of explaining himself. By being unclear, he was telling her he needed help. His symptom—his contradictory message—alerted her to his need for assistance in sharing his true feelings. Not the best solution to his problem, but a solution nonetheless.

Frank's contradiction, as it happened, gave Jill more options for her own behavior. She could choose to respond to both of Frank's messages, or she could acknowledge only one. If, for example, she took his words at face value, she would go ahead and make her vacation plans without regard for his wishes. He had told her to do precisely that. I imagine, though, that Frank would have found some way to sabotage these arrangements, because he really didn't want her to make the plans on her own. But she would be well within her rights to do precisely that— at least as far as his verbal communication went. Or she could attend only to his nonverbal communication, pursuing his emotional state. This response also seemed doomed to failure, as Frank was not able to acknowledge that he was "tight." Jill had a difficult choice to make: should she listen to his words or heed his actions? Her decision would have consequences, not only in this interchange, but in their future discussions.

Jill looked at me, silently asking for help. I assumed that she wanted me to pursue Frank, to show him why she was confused, to confront the discrepancy between his words and the way he was saying them. But I knew that they didn't need to learn to communicate with me; that was relatively easy. They needed to be able to talk to each other. By this time I had seen Jill and Frank communicate for several weeks. They had worked well on other issues, and I wondered why this situation was creating such problems. What was it about vacation plans that made this couple so stressed? I coached them along.

"Jill, what's bothering you?" I asked. "You look confused." I was telling her to ask Frank what he was trying to tell her, and I was also telling them both that it was permissible to use nonverbal cues.

Jill turned her gaze from her husband and looked at me. As though he were suddenly absent, she said, "Frank seems upset. Do you know why he's mad?" I instructed her to tell Frank why she thought he was angry and to ask him why. So she turned to her husband. He was still looking out the window. "Frank," she began in a supplicating voice, "if you don't want to go to my mom's, we don't have to. We can go to your mom's. Would you prefer that?"

I stopped them. Jill had changed her question about Frank's mood into a solution. Frank hadn't even admitted that he was upset, and she was accommodating him. This was communication at its worst! Instead of each of the Curdys explaining his and her feelings and desires, Jill was interpreting Frank's cues and coming up with a solution—a solution that allowed him to avoid even acknowledging his own needs. She was doing the emotional work in the marriage, based on her interpretation of his unstated needs. This was not going to work.

Why doesn't it work when one partner interprets for the other? The answer is both simple and complicated. Simply, for Jill to do Frank's talking for him would put her in the untenable position of arguing against her own wishes. She wanted to go to her family's home at Christmas. Why should she deny herself, especially given his refusal to speak for himself?

On a more complex level, if Jill interprets for Frank, she not only subverts her own desires; she also implies that she is better able to understand his internal reality than he is. She says, by implication, that he cannot speak for himself (rather than that he chooses not to speak for himself) and that she can speak for him. Imagine how this upsets the balance of power in an intimate relationship. Frank has, in choosing to be emotionally mute, demanded that she speak for him. But how can she know what to say? And why should she?

Communication is power. In all areas of our culture, people who get their ideas across are able to affect others. Politicians who can convince the electorate get elected. Bank robbers who can communicate get the money. It is powerful to speak for yourself and to make yourself heard. Clear, effective communication helps us impress others. Saying what you want increases dramatically your chances of getting it.

EXERCISE 8: Imagine an area of discussion that you and your partner negotiate well. It doesn't have to be difficult, just successful. It might be a simple decision, like what weekend plans to make, or a more important issue, like dividing up household chores. What helps you discuss this as well as you do? What aspects of your behavior keep you on track in this area?

Interestingly, poor communication is also powerful. Time and time again, I see individuals refuse to say what they mean, leaving their partners to play Twenty Questions in a vain attempt to please them. People who cannot—or will not—speak for themselves usually have partners who are willing to pursue them. In fact, this "emotional muteness" is almost always a demand that the other person try to find out what you're feeling. Somehow in this game the silent partner needs to be pursued to feel loved.

Often, we do our worst communicating when we are most careful about our partner's feelings. If my husband asks what I want for dinner and I say "I don't care," the chances are that I'm trying to give him the choice. But I'm not communicating clearly. I'm trying to be nice, but I'm being indirect. A clearer communication might be "I want you to pick, because I want you to be happy, and it really doesn't matter to me," or even "I want you to pick, because I don't want to decide."

EXERCISE 9: Now imagine an area where you and your mate are indirect and inefficient. How is this scenario different from the previous one? What is it that doesn't work? Have you tried to change the pattern? How?

When I see a couple with a wide disparity in their emotional expressiveness, I often use an analogy to talk about the power of muteness. Because we are, indeed, at our most powerful when we are most helpless—in our infancy. Think about it: a baby can do nothing for herself, but when she cries, powerful, large adults desperately strive to interpret and meet her needs. Helpless adults can inspire the same desperation in their partners. So the most helpless may be the most powerful! Jill's reaction to Frank indicated that they were relying on this paradigm: she was trying to fix a situation that he could not even admit was causing a problem.

As their therapist, I wanted each individual to speak for himself or herself. I wanted them both to have the freedom to use all parts of their communication to understand each other's meanings. Jill needed to confront the mixed messages she was receiving, and Frank needed to articulate his feelings without subverting his message. That way, true communication could take place.

Who, What, When, Where, and How

One way to understand the patterns of our communication is to look at these sequences through an objective framework. I find the following five aspects of any communication exchange useful in understanding what happens when people try to talk to each other.

WHO is the object of our communication? All communication is directed at a person or group of persons, even when we are thinking or talking to ourselves. So every interaction involves a sender and a receiver. It is helpful to be very clear about WHO is involved in your communications. For example, a public kiss is a communication to your partner, but it also involves the people who are witness to the exchange. Kissing a child in public is very different from kissing another adult. Kisses between same-sex adults are different from kisses between opposite-sex adults. All of this information will affect our understanding of a simple event.

WHAT is the message of the communication? What are you trying to say? In our example of the public kiss, is the message one of tenderness, sexuality, or ownership? Each has an explicit meaning, and most messages have hidden meanings as well. The kiss may be telling something to the participants but have a different meaning for the witnesses.

WHEN does the communication take place? Obviously, the timing of any interaction will influence its effect. Our public kiss is interpreted one way if it occurs first thing in the morning, another way late at night, and yet another in the middle of a fight. It has one meaning if it happens during an X-rated movie, another after a frightening medical diagnosis.

WHERE does the interaction occur? Airport kisses are more common, and are understood differently, than kisses on the street. A public kiss in a church has implications of marriage that do not exist in a mall.

HOW the communication takes place also shapes our interpretation of its meaning. A chaste peck on the cheek is vastly different from a passionate kiss. The witnesses and participants understand the communication differently, depending on all these factors.

Communication Rules

Each member of a couple brings a personal set of rules about communication to the new relationship—rules concerning when they talk about what, where intimate exchanges occur, who raises which topics. We have rules that establish the importance of certain discussions: do you put down the newspaper or turn off the TV? Do you look at your partner? Does the discussion take place over a meal, in the car, or in passing? Obviously, Jill's decision to raise the topic of vacation plans in my office was a communication in and of itself. Why was she initiating this conversation with Frank in front of me? What did this choice mean to Jill—and to Frank?

One of the ways to understand communication is to break it down into component parts. The Curdys' interchange in my office helps to illustrate these aspects of communication. All parts of any interactive sequence are chock full of important information. We attend to different parts at different times, depending on the situation, the outcome we hope for, and the individuals with whom we are interacting. My job as their therapist was to help the Curdys communicate better, so I listened to different parts of the exchange.

The first aspect I noted was SETTING. As I've said, I was struck that Jill chose to bring up this issue in my office. For many newlyweds, the issue of whose family to vacation with is a loaded one, so Jill's decision to have the conversation in front of me clearly said that it was a hot topic. I was sure that Frank got this message—and it may well have increased his hostility. There may have been an implication that they would be unable to resolve the problem on their own.

EXERCISE 10: For one week, have the "How was your day?" conversation in as many different settings as possible. Talk about it on the phone, over dinner, with other people around, with the TV on, as you're making dinner or are otherwise distracted, in bed. Each of these conversations will feel different, often in very small ways. Notice the differences. Which setting is best for you? Under what circumstances would you prefer a different setting? Your answers may be different from your partner's—and that is very important information! What works for you may not work as well for your partner. Discovering this will help you find ways to talk—even about the most mundane subjects—that are best for both of you.

Another important aspect of communication is TIMING. When we say something often can be as critical as what we say. Do you share good news while you're at work? Do you save your complaints until bedtime? How long had Jill Curdy waited to initiate this conversation? I noted that the Curdys had not decided about their holiday plans—and it was already November. I could guess from my own experience that extended family had been asking about their plans for some time. Why had the couple waited so long to resolve this thorny issue? Whose feelings were so vulnerable? I knew that they had left the decision until almost the last possible date, and that this inevitably would result in more hurt feelings. What kept them from working it through earlier? This was my second clue that the issue of vacation plans was loaded and difficult.

My third clue to the importance of the discussion we were facing was the PHYSICAL CUE each one provided. Jill's anxiety was obvious as she watched Frank for response. His anger was palpable. They looked at me rather than at each other. They stared out the window. They were giving each other every indication that the discussion would not go well.

One of my tasks was to help them respond to the nonverbal cues they were giving each other. They needed to know that this level of communication was important. We often ignore such messages, because they are hard to understand. The Curdys had to incorporate these important bits of information, and I coached them along at the task.

"Frank, you sound angry. I'm confused—you say Jill can decide, but I think you do care about what she decides."

Frank blurted out, "How can I decide what we should do? She's in charge anyhow." Jill looked crestfallen, but I was secretly relieved. Once he articulated his anger, we could work with his words—and that's so much easier! Words require much less interpretation, because their meaning is generally clearer. We know where we stand, most of the time, when we're using words.

Jill tried to placate her angry husband. "I don't mean to be in charge. I'm sorry." This is a pattern I see time and again—a spouse apologizing for some slight that he or she really doesn't understand. Jill had no idea what Frank was complaining about, but she took responsibility for it anyway. Without comprehending his objection, she was ready to be blamed. I asked her what she was sorry for; she looked blank.

This is an impossible situation—responsibility without power. Jill had taken responsibility for the problem, but since she had no understanding of Frank's complaint, she was powerless to make a change. We can be responsible only for those aspects of our lives which we control. We are not responsible for things we cannot change. I had to explain this to the Curdys, but first I had to get Frank to explain his concern to his wife—and get Jill to listen to his complaint without trying to fix it immediately. This was, after all, Frank's complaint, not Jill's. He was responsible—and entitled—to fix his own problem.

"In charge?" I asked.

"Yes," he said quietly as he shook his leg rapidly. He shifted in his seat. "She makes all the decisions. Where we live, who we see, what's for dinner. I'm just there to keep her company."

Suddenly, Jill entered the fray. "Sure I do. What do you ever decide? Nothing matters enough to you for you to participate.

You just like to complain about my decisions!" This conversation felt different to me. We weren't just talking about vacation now—we were talking about decision-making. I knew the topic was meatier, more central for the Curdys. Frank glared at his matronly wife. She glared back.

The Curdys were communicating now. But were they listening? And what were they actually saying?

It is obvious that listening is an essential part of communication. Most of us focus on what needs saying, but what needs hearing is equally critical. Each of the Curdys was telling the partner something important, but the discussion was at a high emotional level, and neither was listening. This is the kind of conversation that almost seems to be tape-recorded. Each person speaks in predictable ways, with a predictable response, and nothing seems to change. The talks are very frustrating for couples. We feel that we have said something central, important, and our partner doesn't pick up on even the simplest part. Instead, he continues to make his own point without hearing the true meaning of our position.

All couples have such tape-recorded fights. In fact, these quarrels often serve an important purpose: they help us extricate ourselves from other, more serious problems. We go to these quarrels when the problem we should be focusing on is too difficult or too scary. That's why most of our awful fights end the same way—because we choose to argue in this less dangerous fashion. Tape-recorded fights are less risky—because we know how they will turn out.

As soon as the Curdys' voices were raised, both stopped listening. The fourth aspect of communication is DECIBEL LEVEL. In fact, those essential messages—the ones we say loudly to guarantee that we'll be heard—were the very communications they could not hear. Most messages delivered loudly are not heard. It is a strange part of human nature that we often share our most important ideas in a way that ensures their being ignored!

I stopped Frank and Jill. "This feels like a fight you've had before. I'll bet each one of you knows exactly what the other one is going to say next." They laughed sheepishly. "Let's try to do this differently. Frank, try to tell Jill what you want."

"I want her to leave me alone about these plans. I want her to stop trying to involve me. She's going to decide anyhow!"

I held up my hand to Jill, who was champing at the bit to rebut his accusation. It would have been more of the same, and I wanted to change the pattern. "No, Frank. That's what you *don't* want. I want you to tell her what you *do* want." He paused, not certain how to answer. I spoke again. "It's like going into a restaurant and telling the waiter that you don't want chicken. How do you know what he'll bring you? So we tell the waiter what we do want—and we expect just that! If you tell Jill what you want, you radically increase your chances of getting it."

This is a surprisingly difficult concept for couples. Asking for what we want seems to indicate that we've somehow failed, that our partner doesn't simply know what we want. For newlyweds, it may feel like abandonment. We think that our spouse should understand automatically what we want, that understanding is part of love. It's not. Just because someone loves you does not mean she can understand you. It means that she will *try* to understand you, that she is concerned about you, that she will listen to you explain yourself. *But not that she can read your mind.* For many, grasping this is one of the first giant steps toward a real marriage. A real marriage demands partners who are willing to explain themselves to each other—without demanding agreement!

Frank sighed and seemed to gird himself. "Well, I guess I should listen to you. We're paying you 'cause you're supposed to know what you're talking about. Right?" He turned to his wife. "I don't care where we go, because I don't want to go anywhere. I want to be a family of just us. I want to have holidays at our house—not with your family or my family. And I know you won't allow that. So why should I even get involved?"

Frank, anticipating Jill's refusal to celebrate holidays at home, had decided that the subject was not even worth pursuing. In effect, he made it impossible to get his own needs acknowledged, much less met. He denied her the opportunity to respond to his wishes.

I turned to Jill, who looked as if she'd been hit by a train; she was a funny combination of pale and red, quiet and angry. I wondered whether she was going to destroy him with her next words. But they surprised me. A smile began to break on her face, followed by a grin on his. Within seconds, the Curdys were laughing.

"That was the problem? Frank, what an idiot you are," Jill teased.

"OK, OK! So I'm an idiot. I thought you wanted to go home."

"I do. And we will. But let's do something at our house, too. Let's work it out so we're an 'us' and a part of them. Why didn't you tell me?"

The Curdys were doing well. They had begun to solve the immediate situation, and Jill had followed up with a question about the larger problem—what had kept Frank from making his wishes known?

He looked away. Was he angry or embarrassed? Both? "I don't know what it is. I guess I know you'll work it out. Like you just did. I mean, I told you what I wanted and you came up with a compromise between what I want and what you want. Just like that. I guess I know you'll fix it, regardless of what I say."

This was an important leap in their conversation. They had moved from a simple, concrete problem to a larger, more involved, emotion-laden issue. This often happens in the best communication sequences. We make the transition from a topic of discussion (what shall we do for the holidays?) to the rules of that same discussion (who decides and why?). They were no longer negotiating their vacation plans. Instead, the Curdys were talking about talking. And this would yield much more substantial results.

Talking about talking is difficult but productive. It requires trust and history, a sense that a couple is committed to each other over the long haul. It also demands a shared language, refined through experience. In fact, talking about talking is never finished. It is one of the continuing tasks of marriage—to process and improve our communication.

How do couples talk about talking? These extremely productive conversations are the way we set and change the rules of our interactions. However, to have the talks, couples must follow some general ground rules and may need to establish their own rules. These verbal interactions can be fraught with emotion, and they need the protection afforded by regulations.

Talking About Talking

It is difficult to begin talking about talking. There is a danger that such a conversation will deteriorate into a free-for-all, as each individual feels accused. But the discussions can be very helpful.

> EXERCISE 11: What communication rules apply in your relationship? How do you let each other know when an issue is important? How do you communicate your feelings about that issue? Do you confuse the issue with other ideas, or other cues? What are the WHO, WHAT, WHEN, WHERE, and HOW you use to understand your partner's behavior? What clues do you think your partner gives you? Compare notes.

Recognizing patterns based on present cues and our individual historical communication patterns is important. These expectations set a "tolerance level" for all aspects of a relationship—from the degree of intimacy to the acceptability of physical expressions of anger. When we begin to understand these patterns, we can take control of them and change them as we see fit.

> EXERCISE 12: Think about a time when you felt very close to your partner—even if you did not agree. Try to identify what made this moment so close. How did the conversation begin? What signals did you send and receive? How did you validate your partner's perceptions? How were yours respected? What parts of the communication sequence worked best? Where was there room for improvement?

Talking about talking must take place under neutral circumstances. The worst way to explain a position is when your partner feels under attack. It is essential that both parties to the conversation be prepared—and calm—so that there is equal participation in the discussion. In addition, although it is easy to tell your partner what you dislike, it is not productive. Hearing what's wrong with you doesn't generally make you change; it makes you withdraw. We are much more likely to be happy with the outcome if we tell each other what we do want—not what we don't want. Hearing what your partner wants, whether it's about sex or what's for dinner or how many children to have, always provides areas for discussion.

No solution is cast in stone. Any resolution a couple achieves may create other problems. Couples need to renegotiate decisions, of any kind, over the course of a long marriage. Simply put, people change, so our solutions must change, too. This is part of the journey we call marriage—and it can be a lot of fun. Couples who can enjoy learning and relearning about each other are much more likely to stay happily married. I believe that part of the adventure of love, the excitement of being in a committed relationship, is the fearless exploration of another person—physically and emotionally.

SUGGESTIONS FOR FURTHER THOUGHT

- Think of examples of mixed signals in other relationships with your family, your boss, your best friend. What was confusing? How did you try to understand what message was being sent? When do you send mixed signals? Why?

- Think about how you and your partner talk now. How do you communicate your pleasure and your disappointment? What rules work well for you? Which are less efficient? How can you make changes together?

Cinderella and her prince
have lived very different lives—she sings
with mice, scrubs floors, eats the dregs of her
stepsisters' dinner. He is surrounded by courtiers who
admire him, attends glittering balls, and concerns himself
with affairs of state. How will they behave at their first state
dinner? How will they know how to act toward each other
and toward their respective families? What can she give
him that has value in his belief system? What does he
have to offer her that she will cherish?
How will they know?

4

RITUALS

OUR BEHAVIOR IS DICTATED BY THE RITUALS IN OUR
lives. These rituals may have great importance, such as those
we practice when mourning the loss of our loved ones, or
may appear almost simplistic and unimportant, such as those
we practice in deciding when to go to bed. They help us to lead
our lives in comforting, predictable ways. They help us celebrate
the events of our lives, both sorrowful and joyous.

Think of the many rituals surrounding a wedding. The bride
wears white, and is escorted down the aisle by her father or both
parents. There is "something old, something new, something
borrowed, something blue." Every religion contributes its
unique traditions. The groom stands awaiting his bride at some

kind of altar, even if it's only the desk in the judge's office. There is a celebration afterward, usually with food. People are meant to be happy.

These rituals carry great meaning, even when they contribute nothing to the solemnity of the occasion. At my own wedding, I wanted to have a chocolate cake. My father was appalled at the idea of a chocolate wedding cake! He felt it was not appropriate, that people do not have chocolate in their wedding cakes. And that was that. It was clear to me that the flavor of cake at a wedding was not essential to the meaning of this solemn and joyous occasion. But for my father the flavor was part of the ritual—and an important part. So we did not change his ritualistic idea about the cake; it mattered too much to him.

We have other rituals that we call on more frequently. We say good night to our parents, children, and spouses in special ways. My husband and I say "I love you" each time we end a phone call. We eat certain foods on certain nights of the week, or we call our parents every Sunday at 2 P.M. All of these are ritual behaviors, behaviors that have taken on meaning for us.

We have extensive rituals about holidays. Take Thanksgiving, for example, a holiday replete with ritual behavior. We eat at the same home every year, or we rotate on a schedule, or we go to a hotel. We eat at noon, at 2 P.M., or after the football game. We watch football, or we do not. We watch the parade or attend services. We give thanks to God, or we just eat. Everyone brings food, or the host cooks, or we have the meal catered. We recall the changes of the past year. Children eat with the adults or sit at a separate table. The menu remains the same or is changed in specific ways.

Most families have rituals about other events in their life. Some people have traditional desserts for birthdays, such as ice cream cakes or a special cake that Mommy always makes. In one family, the mother makes a special pie for each birthday, and every year the family struggles about what to make for her birthday. Does she get "Birthday Pie?" Who makes her pie?

Does the family sing "Happy Birthday" or other songs? Are the candles lit in another room and brought, dramatically, to the birthday girl or boy? Does the whole family assist in blowing out the candles, or are the candles extinguished only by the celebrant? How do these rules differ for children and adults? These behaviors, ritualized without our even knowing that they are, influence our perceptions of later events. We see the world through the prism of experience.

It is often confusing to us that such traditions have so much meaning for us and our spouses. Imagine that each family creates a map for behavior. Every member of the family is given the map and learns how to follow it. Over time, however, the family members need the map less and less. They have learned the terrain and can find their way without assistance. Each of us has such a map inside our head. We know what behavior is considered appropriate and acceptable, and what is not. The map is useful, and it works for those who share it. Eventually, the sharers begin to forget that the map ever existed—until a new member joins the family, with a different personalized map inside his or her head.

New People, Old Traditions

The appearance of a new member on the family scene means that the map must be brought out of storage. The new person must be introduced to the family's map, its set of behavioral expectations. Often the process is complicated, as the family may no longer know how to describe its own map. Further, the new member, having brought his or her own internal guidelines to the relationship, will surely want to add some of these traditions to the map. Suddenly, a couple may find themselves arguing about important behaviors, having to justify "doing it my way."

Arguments like these are enormously potent. We care how holidays and other rituals are celebrated. Rituals connect us to our past, and to the past of our people, be it our family, or ethnic, geographic, or economic group. This is why marriages between people from different socioeconomic classes or religious groups may seem shakier than others; there is no assumption of shared ethnic or cultural behavior. Even when we assume a common tradition, we may be surprised by the differences in our rituals.

Simon and Leslie Kaufman had been married for less than a year when they had their first confrontation over ritual. Simon had grown up in an assimilated Jewish family, with grandparents who were Russian immigrants. He was especially close to his grandmother, the family storyteller. She told him magical tales of her parents and siblings, of her childhood in Russia. He especially loved the story of her flight from Russia, being chased by Cossacks across the border. As an adult, he recognizes that she was not only a great storyteller, but a great exaggerator as well. But she was his grandma, and he loves her memory. He is an author, and he says that his stories are a legacy from her and a testament to her love.

Leslie, an accountant, was raised in a loving, intellectual family. Her parents enjoyed arguing about anything and everything. There was no hostility in their discussions, and dinnertime was punctuated by wonderful explorations of thought. She feels blessed by the training she received, the stimulation to think that has helped her throughout her professional and personal life.

Simon and Leslie love to talk, endlessly. They laugh, discuss, debate. They told me that no one could keep up with them, and that no topic was off limits to them. That is, until one holiday time.

Simon and Leslie were both raised in the Jewish faith. One of their most important holidays is Passover, a commemoration of the escape of Hebrew slaves from Egypt five thousand years ago. They both love Passover, with its ancient rhythm and ritual. But their first celebration led to anger and tears.

The couple prepared for the holiday together, discussing each detail. Whom they would invite, what dishes they would serve, where their guests would sit. They had a wonderful time, right up until the seder—the ritual meal—got under way. Then the confusion and anger began. In Leslie's family, the entire group read from the Hagaddah, the book that recounts the story of the Exodus. They went around the room informally, each person reading in order, with interruptions from others who wanted to recite certain passages. In Simon's family, the man sat at the head of the table and read the whole story to an attentive, polite audience. So Simon expected to read and be listened to, to take command in the style of his Russian grandmother as she had expounded her tales from the old country, while Leslie anticipated a lively discussion, with everyone joining in the reading, much like her family's discussions every night. As the evening progressed, they became angrier and more irritated, and finally exploded in rage. The Kaufmans, frightened by their fury, found themselves in my office not more than a week later.

Anger and Avoidance

Leslie, a well-dressed, somewhat formal woman, sat primly at the edge of her seat. I could tell that she was bursting, ready to tell me her story at practically the speed of sound. Simon, much more reserved, sat back and waited as his wife described their first Passover. "He is so controlling," she said indignantly. "He needed to be in charge of everything—and he didn't even want me to read! It was so sexist! This is not the man I thought I married." I could hear both rage and sorrow in her voice: rage at his behavior, sorrow at her ignorance of his potential for overbearing conduct. She felt betrayed by him—not only by his behavior, but by his refusal to understand what he had done wrong or to respond to the intensity of her feeling.

Simon was calm. He quietly described Leslie's rage as "an

overreaction." He told her he had wanted to enthrall her with the Passover story. I suspected that he was very frightened by her rage, and unsure of what his next move should be, but he was unable to tell her how scared he was. So he became more and more "rational," avoiding his fears and her anger by distancing himself from the argument. Not surprisingly, this enraged Leslie further, beyond even her own experience.

The first and most pressing issue to be dealt with was their behavior at the Passover seder, although the problem was primarily symptomatic, rather than a root cause. We talked about their expectations of the seder, about how seders had been conducted in their respective families of origin. Such patterns influence our perception of what behavior should always be, I explained, so we need to know where we come from, rather than assuming that we all share common experiences. We need to tell each other our stories in detail, because the stories reflect our expectations and our hopes.

There was another aspect of ritual behavior that I was witnessing in this couple, one with potentially more serious consequences than the argument about the seder. Both Simon and Leslie were slipping into gender roles. While she became more and more shrill, almost as though the loudness of her voice would convince him that her position was correct, he became more and more detached, denying his own emotional state. Thus, she became "the emotional one," and he became "the reasonable one." She appeared to be intensifying their argument, while he seemed to be trying to control the emotion-ality between them.

Both Simon and Leslie were behaving in ways that produced exactly the opposite effect than intended: her anger, rather than clarifying her feelings to him, actually made Simon back away from the fight. His detachment, rather than calming Leslie so that they could talk about their fight, increased her fury.

Patterns That Work; Patterns That Don't

This is a pattern every therapist sees over and over, a pattern that blocks rather than promotes change. Regardless of who begins this stereotypic interaction, one person withdraws and the other shouts and screams. The first then withdraws more, and the second yells louder. Typically, the man withdraws and the woman does the shouting, but sometimes the pattern is reversed.

I believe that Simon and Leslie were not only behaving like a man and a woman, but were behaving according to the cultural roles prescribed for them by gender. Unconsciously, we all bring these well-learned roles into our relationships. They are, if you will, scripts that tell us how we should behave. We are accomplished at enacting these scripts even without realizing that we are doing so. These are examples of ritual behaviors, often ritualized at a societal level. Women tend to shout or scream, and men tend to withdraw. Women tend to become depressed, and men to become angry. Women tend to withdraw into other relationships, and men to withdraw into work.

These male and female scripts, known as sex-role stereotypes, are often laid out for us at a very young age. They tell us how to behave according to our gender. A girl may be discouraged from her interest in science; a boy may be discouraged from playing with dolls. Girls may be taught to relinquish power; boys may be taught to acquire power at all costs. Our parents, teachers, cultural stories, and expectations tell us how and how not to behave. Some of the lessons are about morality, some are about politeness, some are about gender roles. We usually absorb the lessons without realizing it, because we are taught them at such a young age.

Sometimes sex-role prescriptions can guide us to appropriate behavior. We learn how to act in social and professional situations through custom, although the gender-based stereo-types may limit our range of behaviors. At other times, possibly more frequently, the formulas reduce our options for conduct and emotional expression in ways that may make us less capable and efficient. For although some generalizations about human behavior are based on statistical differences between the sexes, they may not apply to a given man or woman. For example, a woman may be a great engineer, even though women tend to be less mechanical. A man may be a great caretaker, even though we think of caretaking as "woman's work." Sex-role stereotypes predict—and often circumscribe—our actions, rather than allowing us to act in ways that are natural and more productive. It is not true that women are biologically more emotionally expressive, nor is it true that men do not know how they feel, although sex roles would indicate that these are rules. In my practice, I have found that men are quite capable of describing and expressing their own emotions, that women can be reason-able and rational. The sex-role scripts for behavior deny us the ability to be distinctive individuals. If all men behave according to one pattern, then individual men are interchangeable. Obviously, both common sense and experience tell us that people are not fungible; why, then, should our internal scripts tell us differently?

Scripts in Our Relationships

Scripts for appropriate masculine and feminine behavior may have a powerful impact on our intimate relationships. If we believe, if we know, that men and women are "supposed" to behave according to a particular set of rules, we will be disappointed and upset if our partner deviates from them. A man who expects his wife to know instinctively how to be a parent will be shocked if she is unsure or inept. A woman who expects

her husband to "be strong" will be worried, and possibly reject-
ing, if he cries. Each couple must negotiate which parts of
society's scripts fit their own relationship.

When my husband and I were preparing for our wedding, the
rabbi showed us the wedding vows. I was to promise to love and
honor Mike, while he was to love, honor, and protect me. My
husband insisted that I promise to protect him as well—not out
of a feminist vision of the world, but simply because he wants
my protection! Now, I'm not about to fight off muggers or
perform acts of superhuman strength, but I do offer him a great
deal of emotional and psychological protection, as people in
marriages usually do. The rabbi was visibly startled by our
request. He had never thought of the various forms of protection a woman offers a man. I was made aware of this part of our
marital contract by Mike's explicit wish for my promise of
protection.

> EXERCISE 13: Look at the following words. Which
> ones apply more to men? Which apply more to women?
> Compare your answers with your partner's. Do not
> expect that your answers will—or should—be the
> same.
>
> mad, happy, strong, self-sufficient, needy,
> aware, sensitive, dependent, talkative, silent,
> silly, concerned, thoughtful, intelligent,
> independent, creative, mechanical
>
> You may be surprised by some of the answers of you and
> your mate. While there are no right or wrong ones, your
> personal responses may give you some areas for discus-
> sion. You may learn about some of your gender
> expectations—and now you have the opportunity to
> discuss your potentially different perceptions with your
> mate.

The effect of gender roles on a relationship can be quite powerful, particularly if our gender expectations are unspoken. When we begin to know consciously what these scripts are, we can start to change what doesn't work for us. When our rabbi heard my husband describe the kinds of protection I offer him, the rabbi changed his perception of the word *protection*. He no longer saw it only in terms of physical safety, but was able to understand new meanings of the word. I also heard Mike tell me that I need to be careful with him, that he needs me to make his world safer. All three of us stepped out of our gender-based understanding of the word *protection* and learned a new meaning for one aspect of the marital relationship.

Sexual Rituals

Not surprisingly, we not only have rituals about holidays, fighting, and gender roles; we also have rituals about sex. Many couples find that they have a pattern of sexual behavior, whether the pattern covers frequency, initiation behaviors, position. Who gets to have the yearning and how it is communicated is also ritualized. Must both partners want to be sexual, or is one person's need more important? We also have rules for our attitude toward sexuality—is it serious or fun? Do people talk during sex? Do we evaluate our performance afterward? Do we cuddle when we're done, or go about our business separately? And, of course, who is guaranteed an orgasm?

Each couple establishes rules for sexual behavior based on past experience, gender expectations, comfort, and pleasure. These rules are rarely negotiated explicitly, though the partners are usually sharply aware of the rules. Because the parameters of sexual behavior are not clearly discussed, they are often difficult to change. As with sex-role stereotypes, it is important that couples become aware of their rituals for sexual behavior if they want to change the rules.

Remember Larry and Mary Jo, the couple in Chapter 2 whose struggle over separateness and closeness threatened to end their marriage? As they began to explore aspects of their on-and-off relationship, they talked about their sex life. Larry, after long weeks alone on the road, wanted to come home and jump into bed with Mary Jo immediately. He laughed at himself as he described his reaction to seeing his wife again. "I just need some skin! It's less about sex and more about feeling like I'm there. I want to be *THERE.*" It didn't surprise me that this wasn't what Mary Jo wanted. She still needed to see herself as separate and independent, to see him as a part of her life, but not too important a part, to keep her walls up.

"I want him to come home and be happy to just be home. I don't understand why he needs *ME* so much." Their sexual ritual was a part of the home-coming behavior. Larry would "pester" Mary Jo for sex, and she would be irritated by his neediness. He would continue to nag her, and finally she would "give in." They would have sex, which they would both enjoy a great deal. After the sex, she would feel closer to him, and finally be happy that he was once again at home. Their sexual behavior was a critical part of their emotional interaction, allowing her to break down her barriers against him, allowing him to give something to her.

There are clear gender distinctions in sexual behavior. Although such distinctions are, at best, generalizations, it is interesting to note that men and women tend to prefer different parts of the sexual encounter. Most women enjoy foreplay and cuddling more than intercourse; most men prefer intercourse to foreplay. Women are multiorgasmic, while few men are. Obviously, these differences require that couples negotiate which parts of the sexual experience are to be emphasized and for what length of time.

When Rituals Don't Work

Rituals can be wonderful if they serve their purpose. But what happens when they do not, when they are disruptive or uncomfortable? How do people change their rituals? Whether the ritual concerns religion, money, sex, or fighting, changing it is difficult. The mates must become aware, not only of what each one does that irritates the other, but also of what each contributes to the discomfort. The individuals have to understand what expectations they brought to the relationship, and which of these expectations are helpful. Each must listen to the mate, hearing what the other one wants and needs—and why. Each must understand the intended purpose of the ritual behavior. For this reason, Larry and Mary Jo needed to explore how their sexual ritual brought them back "in touch" with each other. Simon and Leslie, on the other hand, needed to study the history of their differing expectations so that they could negotiate a different approach, one that would work for both of them, leaving neither out.

EXERCISE 14: Describe a typical birthday celebration in your original family. Was the cake store-bought or homemade? Were presents purchased or hand-made? Did you eat cake before or after giving the presents? Were the lights on or off as the cake was brought into the room? How were people expected to react to presents and cake? What songs did you sing? Did you write thank-yous, or say them, or were they considered unnecessary? Whose birthdays were celebrated? Whose were ignored? Did you get or send cards?

Which parts of this ritual do you wish to continue? Which would you prefer to dispense with? Which parts of your ritual are essential to the celebration of a birthday? After you know what you *need* and what you could change, discuss with your spouse how the two of you would like to celebrate birthdays.

Rituals bring us together, make us feel part of a relationship. They teach us about appropriate behavior and help us evaluate others. They can be the glue that keeps us together in difficult times, sustaining people in shaky relationships until issues can be safely addressed and resolved. We can thrive on rituals, using them to communicate love and caring, even when we must be harsh and critical. Human relationships would not survive without rituals, but our rituals must serve the relationship. If we do otherwise, if our relationships serve our rituals, then we may lose the relationship. Rituals should strengthen and give meaning to love and caring, but should not define love and caring.

SUGGESTIONS FOR FURTHER THOUGHT

- Think of a private ritual you enjoy, of another that is particular to your family of origin, and a cultural ritual. Compare these to your partner's.
- Talk about the rituals you might institute as a couple, such as Sunday night dinners, anniversary celebrations. How could these rituals serve your relationship?
- Talk about the rituals you have implemented without thinking: she does the dishes; he takes out the trash; we eat with the TV on. Are you comfortable with these choices? Can they be changed?

Prince Charming and Cinderella are probably the same religion, but they worship God in very different ways. He prays in a huge Church, with gold and silver all around. She prays at home with her mice. He donates to the Church, and has an important role in religious ceremony. She has little experience with formal religion, and is probably uneducated. How do they integrate their beliefs and practices?

5

RELIGION

IN OUR INCREASINGLY OPEN AND MOBILE SOCIETY, couples frequently come from vastly different backgrounds. We have been taught that all people are created equal, that we should not limit our social circle to those exactly like ourselves. Because of this widened contact, there has been a rise in interclass, interfaith, and interracial marriages. We are no longer limited to our own "kind," and this can bring surprises to young couples.

Relationships that cross formerly unquestioned boundaries must forge new rules in the changed society. Couples must establish practices for raising children with different traditions, for dealing with in-laws of another race, faith, or social class.

They must deal with the social disapproval that may follow the unorthodox choice.

In my psychology practice, I have worked with many interfaith couples. Such relationships can present special problems that the couples have to address up front. Issues with in-laws may be exacerbated; many couples want to resolve the question of their future children's religion. All such issues can change the nature of early marriage.

Why is religion so important? For many of us, it has a small place in our daily lives. We may observe the essential holidays of our faith, celebrating only those which have meaning for us. We may even declare we practice the bits we do only because it's important to our parents, our families. Many of us have little sense of ownership of our religion, and little commitment. Religion is often a side issue in our very busy lives.

But even for the relatively nonobservant, religion is more than a simple set of God beliefs. It's more than the Holy Trinity or the Passover seder. It is also a set of traditions, guidelines for our holiday celebrations, for childrearing, and for acknowledging life's celebrations and losses.

Even the secular traditions of religion take on important meaning. Imagine a woman whose family exchanged Christmas presents on Christmas morning. Her new husband gives her a Christmas present on Christmas Eve, his family's traditional time for gift-giving. While she may like her present and the thought that went into its choice, she may feel disappointed, as if something is missing, when she awakens on Christmas Day to a tree barren of presents. We expect to repeat what we've grown up with, and we feel a sense of loss when these expectations go unmet.

Traditions take on even more importance when the couple comes from different religions. A person whose belief system includes a personal relationship with Jesus, for example, must make a huge leap to live with a person who doesn't believe in Jesus as the son of God. And, unlike other areas of our relationships, it's almost impossible to come up with a compromise in the area of religion.

How can couples work with disparate religious beliefs? For many the issue doesn't arise until the couple begins to plan their future together. We are respectful of our individual differences and may even share in each other's holidays, but a couple is faced with the need to make decisions when they plan a wedding, marriage, and children.

Marjorie Bonner and Frank Tedesco had been dating for two years when they began to talk about marriage. Marjorie, a Southern Baptist, and Frank, a Catholic, met in the small accounting firm where both worked, and became close friends. Soon they were going out for dinner after work. Dinner led to dating and love.

Marjorie called me after speaking with her minister before his first premarital meeting with the two of them. The minister, who had known the Bonner family all Marjorie's life, listed some potential problems in the interfaith relationship. Marjorie told me she felt betrayed by his pessimism. When she talked to Frank about it, he suggested his priest marry them. She was shocked at this idea, shocked and angry.

They came together to see me two days later. Frank, a small wiry man, had his arm protectively around the stiff back of his fiancée. She sat primly on the couch and began to explain. "I can't get married in the Catholic church. My family would be so uncomfortable, and I can't have a mass, and I especially can't sign papers saying that my kids will be Catholic. What about my family and my history and my beliefs?"

"It was only a suggestion," countered Frank. "We can get married anywhere you want. In your church, in mine, in a judge's office. I don't care."

"But it matters. It's how we say our vows—in front of God."

"God's with us in any of those places."

"No, it's not that simple. What religion will we be? And what will our kids be?"

Frank and Marjorie were talking about two different things. Frank was talking about the location of their wedding. Marjorie had moved on from this issue; she was talking about their relationship with religion, as a couple.

These are very important questions. Every couple begins to answer them when they choose a location and officiant for their wedding. In some sense, the choice we make for our wedding sets the tone for future decisions. A couple whose wedding is secular is making a statement not only about their wedding but also about their marriage.

EXERCISE 15: Think back to who married you. Who married your parents, your siblings, your friends? Where were you married? Was this important to you? What religious traditions were part of your wedding? Why?

We may have very deep feelings about our religious traditions. Often, even those who feel little need or connection to religion in daily life try to incorporate religious rituals into the important events of their lives: birth, marriage, childrearing, death. When their traditions are different, partners have to evaluate what really matters to them.

Marjorie Bonner was beginning to make such decisions. She knew that she could not be married in a Catholic church, but she knew that she had to be married in a church. Where did this leave Frank? He continued, "Honey, I really don't care where we're married. The Catholic church means less to me than your church means to you. I know that. But I want to have a party, a real reception. If we get married in a Southern Baptist ceremony, can we have a party, with dancing and drinking? I want to have fun at our reception!"

"What about the minister? My parents? My grandparents?" asked Marjorie. "We can always have a party later for our friends, but I don't want my family to be uncomfortable." Marjorie wasn't arguing that Frank needed to be a Southern Baptist; only that he needed to act like a Southern Baptist on their wedding day. I wondered how he would respond.

"But that's not me. And it's not my family. And it's not us! Why do we have to put on a show? I don't want to do that!" He was getting angry and loud.

Marjorie took a deep breath. "Because we have to. I won't make my family uncomfortable." This sounded like an ultimatum, so I intervened. Ultimatums never go anywhere.

"So you want a Southern Baptist wedding, Marjorie?" I asked. She nodded. "Do you also want a Southern Baptist home?" The wedding is only one day out of a couple's life together. The more important question had to do with their home and how they were going to practice religion jointly—or separately.

"I think so." She looked at Frank, hopefully.

"What does that mean? What is a Southern Baptist home?" Frank's face showed his surprise and confusion.

"Like my parents' home."

"Really? You want no alcohol, no dancing? But you love to dance and party!"

"I know I do. But I don't think you can tell kids that those things are wrong if you do them yourself. So we have to stop."

Frank looked shocked. Marjorie was radically changing the rules, and he wasn't sure what he thought about that. "No beer during football season? No loud parties? No wine with dinner?"

"Not at home." She sounded firm and sure.

"That's not fair. You're imposing your parents' values on us—and we've never lived that way!"

"I know. But marriage is more serious. If we get married, we have to act like adults."

Marjorie and Frank were facing the impact of their different religious traditions head-on. They were beginning to understand what religion meant to both of them so that they could start to make plans for their religious life and the religious life of their family.

"Back up," I suggested. "Tell me about your family's religion and practice." I looked at Marjorie, so she went first. She described a home where God and religion were ever present. There were prayers at every meal, church attendance, volunteer work through the Southern Baptist organization. Her childhood friends were members of the church. Her parents lived an insular life, where everything revolved around the church and its teachings.

I looked at Frank. "My family was very different," he said. "We celebrated Christmas and Easter, of course, and the kids went to CCD. But I knew my parents disagreed with some of the church's teachings, so there were aspects of Catholicism we just ignored."

"But I don't want that," protested Marjorie. "I want our kids to have a real home in the church."

"Even when the church makes silly rules?" Frank clearly thought she was going too far.

"Yes," she answered slowly. "Even when it's silly."

Marjorie was in a place many of us will recognize. She wanted to create a home for Frank and herself within her church. She needed to have a clear religious tradition in her family. And she was comfortable with the beliefs of the Southern Baptist church—even those traditions which meant nothing to her personally.

Religion has deep meaning for many of us. It represents home and family and history. It represents love. We cannot imagine our lives without the rituals and traditions of our family—and these include religion. For most Christians, a house without a Christmas tree is unthinkable. For most Jews, a house with a Christmas tree is equally unthinkable. How can a couple resolve these differences?

EXERCISE 16: Describe an important religious ritual in your original family. How was it celebrated? How often? Who was present? Was there special food?

Special guests? Special clothing? Where was the ritual celebrated? How do you want to incorporate this into your married life? What reaction do you imagine your partner will have?

Some of our rituals are small and seemingly inconsequential. One couple I knew through an interfaith couples' group struggled about the placement of a cross in their bedroom. The cross was a family heirloom, one that had been passed from mother to daughter through many generations. When the couple married, the wife assumed she would receive the cross, and that she would put it in a place of honor over the marital bed. Her Jewish husband was very upset. He couldn't imagine sleeping under a cross. They tried to reach a compromise over its placement, but there was no place in their room where he could tolerate it. It ended up in their guest room, removed every time his parents came to visit. She was resentful and angry at this solution, and it came up often in their religious disagreements. This was a family tradition that was ignored, with unhappy consequences. But the husband had had no idea his new wife would ever expect him to hang a cross over his bed!

Life-Cycle Issues

Religion is most important during life-cycle events. These events are the markers of our lives—birth, death, child rearing, marriage. They are the moments in our lives when we tend to call upon the comfort and structure of our religious traditions for hope, caring, and direction. Small wonder that they are also the times of greatest stress for interfaith couples.

What are these issues? I think there are three major life-cycle issues and an additional one. The three life-cycle issues are marriage, children, and death. The added issue is the continuing relationship with parents. Couples often see their parents and in-laws as their worst problem, because the older generation brings the interfaith issues to the forefront. Mom and Dad are far from shy in posing questions the young couple may wish to avoid— what will the children be, who will marry you, and will you convert? If the couple has decided to postpone these decisions, the parents may require confrontation, with frightening and potentially damaging consequences. Parents and in-laws need answers to unanswerable questions.

These are reasonable, if intrusive, requests. The topics raised by parents are important issues, issues that the young couple must address. In fact, I think that the couple must revisit these concerns throughout their marriage, solving and resolving problems as they arise. While I understand the couple's desire to deal with their relationship on their own, I always validate the parents concerns. How is the couple going to resolve issues of marriage, childrearing, and death?

Marriage

Who will marry an interfaith couple? Many clergy will not co-officiate, so the young couple may be forced to choose between one religion and a secular ceremony. I think that couples are well served by clergy who demand a choice. It is confusing to be married under the rubrics of two religions, especially if they hold strongly differing views on any important aspect. I believe that the couple must begin to choose a house religion as early as possible, rather than waiting for a blowup about the faith of the children.

A house religion? That's similar to the house wine at a restaurant. It is, in some sense, the fallback position. The house religion is what the family follows, apart from previously agreed-on exceptions. So Marjorie and Frank could have decided that their home was Southern Baptist or Catholic—but not both. There may be times when the second religion would take precedence, but the overall expectation was for one religion.

This idea of a house religion allows individuals and couples to have clearly articulated expectations. If Frank agreed, for example, that his home was to be a Southern Baptist home, he would not be surprised at the ban on alcohol and dancing. The issue would be visited once—and would not need to be revisited with any frequency. If Marjorie agreed that their home was to be Catholic, she could stipulate that they not drink with her parents, but would accept that there would be alcohol in their home. Clearly described expectations permit easier adaptation. And a house religion makes childrearing decisions easier, less emotionally loaded.

Children

There is no doubt that children are better served if they are raised in a single religion; they need the simplicity of such an upbringing. They need the self-definition that comes with one faith. And they need to know that their faith is acceptable to Mommy and Daddy.

I have known many couples unable to decide what religion their children will be. They often embrace the idea that they will raise children with knowledge of two religions, and assume that the child will choose his or her religion when older. While I understand that this compromise can work for the adults, I know it to be impossible for children. Parents cannot expect their child to make a choice that they have been incapable of making; they cannot expect the child, as a young adult or even sooner, to create a compromise that should have been made by the parents. Nor should they ask the child to choose between the faiths of Mom and Dad—to choose, that is, between Mom and Dad.

Couples are often surprised that they have such emotional

reactions to this decision. The choice of the child's religion has great meaning to the adults who will raise that child because it represents continuity with their past, with their parents. It represents history and connection. And it gives them the opportunity to re-create important aspects of their own childhood for their children.

> EXERCISE 17: What are your most powerful religious memories of childhood? Do they involve holiday celebration, church or synagogue attendance, family gatherings? How would you like to reproduce these memories in your new family? Which memories do you want to give your children?

One of the ways we re-create our stories and history is to build the same memories for our children. So we may want to have the same decorations on the Christmas tree, or Easter eggs, or celebrate Hanukkah as our family of origin did. These are acts of tradition and history—and they are acts of love, both for our original family and for the family we have created. It is difficult to be asked not to pass on our traditions to our children. It is, in effect, a loss, a death.

The mourning that is part of giving up the chain of religious history may be minor for some people, but it is excruciating for others. They miss the joy of handing on their meaningful rituals. So the woman who wanted the cross over her bed was not only giving up her religious icon; she was also breaking with an important family tradition. It isn't surprising that it hurt her; it does hurt when we split from our past.

Death and Burial

In the final break, death, religion again becomes crucial. As we approach the loss of our loved ones, and as we approach our own mortality, many of us return to the religion of our childhood, with its comforting rhythm and tradition. One man whose wife and children were Jewish realized, after his father's death, that he had broken his link to his father's religious past. He needed to re-create this link, so he and his wife had a late-in-life baby and raised the child in the father's religion, different from that of his mother and his siblings. I often wondered how the parents explained this dichotomy to all the children.

Death raises other important issues for interfaith couples. Some religious traditions allow only people of that faith to be buried in their cemeteries, so spouses of different faiths may not be buried together, with their children, or with their parents.

Death is also a time when traditions are comforting and reassuring. When an individual mourns in an unfamiliar way, the mourning will feel incomplete and false. The rhythm of loss and life will be disrupted, exacerbating the pain of the death. Every religion has significant mourning rituals, which help us say good-bye in familiar ways.

Religion brings us a sense of "home" in times of chaos. While we may overlook the importance of religion and its traditions at happy times, we are usually keenly aware of our religious connections at sad times. And we become increasingly connected to religion as we age.

Joseph Klein and Sally Oman came to see me, not in traditional therapy, but as members of the group for interfaith couples that I ran through a local synagogue. Joseph was a dark and intense man, the oldest child of Holocaust survivors. His parents had met after the liberation of the concentration camps, in a camp for DPs (displaced persons). They emigrated to Israel and then to the United States. Joseph was born on the boat carrying his parents across the Atlantic Ocean, and his parents called him their "future." For them, he represented their triumph over Hitler and the Nazis, over anti-Semitism, over the horrors of the Holocaust. Each was the only survivor of his and her family, and Joseph carried this responsibility on his shoulders; he was both their past and their future.

Joseph's parents settled in the Midwest, in a community with other survivors. He grew up in a primarily Jewish environment, with the smells and sounds of Eastern Europe mingling with his life as an American boy, soon the older brother to two sisters. He straddled both cultures, but found himself yearning to be simply "American," like the other boys. He loved his own religion but hated the feeling of being different.

Sally, a petite woman, had grown up in a large family of Scandinavian descent. Her family had emigrated to the United States five generations back and had settled in a Minnesota farming community full of other Scandinavian Protestant families of hard-working farmers. She was the youngest child in a family of strapping boys, always trying to keep up with her brothers. She described her family as close and caring, the parents focused on the children. They were formal, but loving and concerned.

Sally and Joseph met at college, during their first experience away from their respective nests. They were immediately attracted to each other and described themselves as "kindred souls." Sally loved Joseph's intensity, his attentiveness, his love of learning. He was, she felt, the first person who ever really stopped to listen to her. She felt special and important. Joseph thought Sally the most interesting person he had ever met, with her explorations of herself and her thoughts about her place in the world. He admired her rootedness, her sense of belonging.

Joseph and Sally were aware of their religious differences and concerned about the possible effect on their relationship. Sally's parents and the minister at her church felt the differences were relatively unimportant, as long as Joseph agreed that the young couple could spend holidays with Sally's family. Her parents accepted their relationship, emphasizing the love between the pair over any potential problems caused by their different backgrounds. Joseph's parents, however, were a different story.

The Kleins, now in their mid-sixties, were unhappy with the news that Joseph and Sally were thinking about marriage. They flew to Dallas, where the couple lived, and spoke with their son and his girlfriend at length. The older couple felt close to Sally and decided to be open about their concerns. Sally and Joseph, upset by his parents' "rejection" of their relationship, joined our interfaith group, looking for a place to talk about their feelings.

What were the issues here? This couple, brought together by love and committed to each other, had one set of parents with serious objections to their relationship. The concerns were based on a need for Jewish continuity, a hope that the Judaism almost eradicated by Hitler would outlast this generation into the next. Although the Kleins tried to explain to Joseph and Sally that their reluctance was not a rejection of Sally, the younger couple still felt hurt and angry. My task, and the task of the entire interfaith group, was to help them explore their feelings about their religious differences, to assist them as they tried to make sense of the Kleins' objections, and to enable them to achieve a greater understanding of their choices as they faced the future together or apart.

I also believe this issue was more than one of interfaith differences; the couple was confronting parental objection, perhaps for the first time in their lives. They had to come to terms not only with their own feelings about the issues raised by Joseph's parents, but with their relationship with Joseph's parents, and make decisions about their future. Whose religious tradition was stronger? How would they accommodate to their different needs, especially when they had to decide about the religion of their children? Joseph and Sally each had to look at his and her religious tradition and decide what role it played at present, as well as imagining what role it might play in the future.

We spent hours together, listening to their anger and sorrow. Both were furious at Joseph's parents, who had forced them to confront an issue they felt they could easily table. They were sad that their wonderful relationship was found lacking by such important people. After some time, however, they began to look at the issues raised by the Kleins, and their concern increased. What *were* they going to do?

As they talked, Joseph and Sally began to realize the importance of their religious backgrounds. Sally felt a personal connection to Jesus, a connection Joseph had difficulty understanding. Joseph felt a deep need for Jewish continuity, an obligation to raise Jewish children. Sally, who saw Joseph as a relatively uncommitted Jew, was confused by his powerful insistence on his religion for their children. They struggled together, with the prodding and help of the group. Their conversations, which had previously focused on how surprisingly awful his parents were, took a different path. They realized the issue would be a part of their lives together forever. They needed to learn more about each other's background, religion, and needs. They talked about children and about who would officiate at their marriage. They went to church and to temple. They met with ministers and rabbis. They learned together about Judaism and Christianity, about the rules and expectations each religion imposes on its adherents. They read and studied, talked and cried. Later, when the group sessions were over, they came to meet with me. We sat in my office, pleased to see each other again, ready to restart the struggle for understanding.

Sally began to talk. "I never thought they could have been right." We all knew she was talking about the Kleins. "I thought that love mattered more than differences, but that overlooks the importance of who we each really are. Lots of what I love about Joseph, at least in his mind, comes from the fact that he is Jewish. He thinks his love of learning, of tradition, is all because he's Jewish. I can accept that. But it's hard for me to accept that my kids—whenever we have kids—can't know what I am as well. It's just not fair! I want to give them Christmas and Easter and my family traditions. I like Joe's traditions, and his family is OK. But I want a place in their lives, too. What's wrong with that?"

Joseph was silent. He looked at his hands as she spoke. Sadly, he said, "I hate this. I'm hurting Sally, and I love her. I can't understand why this matters so much to me. If anything, I want these kids, these theoretical kids, to fit in ways that I couldn't. But I need them to be like me, like my parents, like the grandparents the Nazis killed."

Sally was angry. "I don't want children who are Jewish as a memorial to your dead relatives! That's not *my* history! I don't want my children to be the victims of Hitler! What's wrong with my history?" Her voice softened. "Do you think they're in danger from people like me?" This question revealed a great deal of Sally's fear. She was apprehensive that Joseph might see her as so different from himself that he couldn't trust her. For Sally, with her need to be important and to be understood, the idea that Joseph might not trust her was too much to bear.

"Oh, no, babe! I love you! But you can't know what it's like to be Jewish. You can't know how important it is that I give this to our children, that I beat Hitler by making more Jewish babies. There's a number on my mom's arm that tells me to be proud I'm a Jew. How can I overlook what she went through?" For Joseph, this issue was not negotiable. I could see that, and Sally could see that. To have non-Jewish children was more than he could stand. But what would they do? What about Sally's needs? Did she have to concede completely to his greater need, or could they work out a compromise? And—maybe most important to me as their therapist—how would they negotiate this thorny issue while still being caring and respectful of their differences?

We talked about these issues for months. I pointed out that in other areas where they were different, they tried to explain their feelings to each other. In this area, Joseph felt that Sally would never understand his feelings, so he had quit trying to explain himself. He began to talk again, and she began to understand. They went to Holocaust memorials and asked his parents to tell them their stories. They talked to each other and to other interfaith couples. They attended a course on Judaism, where Joseph felt he learned as much as Sally did. She began to make proposals about having a Jewish home, and spoke with her parents at length about how they would feel toward Jewish grandchildren. Joseph laughed at her commitment to having a home with religion, but he was secretly relieved.

Over time, Sally felt a need not only to know about Judaism, but to practice what she knew. While she was not ready to become Jewish, she began to bring Jewish ritual into their home, lighting candles on Friday night and attending services at the synagogue. She demanded that they spend Christian holidays with her family so that she would not lose all that she was, but she understood that he did not want to celebrate these holidays in their own house. She pushed Joseph to a greater understanding of his own background and felt increasingly comfortable with his parents. After a while she told him his parents' objections had been a gift. Joseph and Sally, able to listen to the very real concerns of the Kleins, overcame an important obstacle in their relationship. The skills they learned and the patterns they established would help them in the future. Their relationship with the Kleins was improved. When they decided to marry, they received the blessings of both families.

Sally and Joseph confronted the issues raised by the elder Kleins. They began by being angry at his parents for criticizing their love, but moved to an understanding that these were issues for them as well. Ultimately Joseph acknowledged his connection to his Judaism, and Sally mourned what she would have to give up. They found ways to work with both sets of parents and to create a new life together.

It Keeps on Changing

It is essential that all couples know that this issue, like other important ones in marriage, will not be negotiated only once. Our needs change over time, as our lives change. We may have an expanded need for religion, or we may reject God and organized worship. Life will shock us toward observance or push us away. We will all change as individuals, and this will produce a new marital relationship.

Religious negotiations are often emotionally difficult. We must be patient and understanding, accepting the need for ongoing discussion and respectful of our changing feelings. We must allow our needs to change and must make room for our partner's growth.

SUGGESTIONS FOR FURTHER THOUGHT

- How are your religious traditions different from your partner's? Even if you share the same religion, don't assume that your traditions are identical.

- Which traditions are important to you? Which are less important?

- How have you and your partner negotiated religious practices?

- Think about your expectations for the religion of your home. Have you explained to your partner what you want?

The king meets Cinderella's stepmother and stepsisters. They are not the same kind of people, to say the least. And yet they are suddenly family. How can he accept this orphan and her selfish relatives? How can she hold her own with her regal father-in-law?

6

IN-LAWS

ONE OF THE MOST STRESSFUL AREAS A COUPLE must negotiate as they begin their marital journey is their relationship with each extended family. Our popular culture is rife with stories of difficult in-laws—in-laws who are demanding or degrading, in-laws who cannot leave the couple alone, in-laws who expect constant phone calls and family meals. Most couples have difficulty figuring out whose family to spend Easter or Thanksgiving with, and struggle with hurt feelings and disappointed expectations. The biblical injunction "Therefore shall a man leave his father and his mother, and shall cleave unto his wife: and they shall be one flesh" (Genesis 2:24) is easier said than done. Both the couple and the extended family will struggle as the transition is made, if it is made at all.

Historically, marital choice was a simple matter. Parents, usually fathers, picked their children's spouses, based on dowry, background, and earning capacity. Issues of love and compatibility were subjugated to other, often economic, concerns. Spouses may not have met before their wedding date was set, or even until the wedding night itself. Imagine the distress we would feel, in today's world, if someone tried to pick our mates for us!

This process is reversed today. Parents no longer pick their child's mate, and the child is no longer obligated to accept parental choice. Rather, the child picks his or her own spouse, and the parents are expected to accept the new person and welcome him or her into the family, without concern, criticism, or question. This is a huge leap for many parents, one they may not be able to make. Suddenly your child, whom you have advised and directed throughout his or her life, has the upper hand in a critical matter. The child brings a new member into your family, and you have no say in the decision!

It is not surprising that so many in-law relationships are fraught with difficulty. Each partner in the marriage is still strongly affiliated with his or her family of origin and wants those people to be happy. But because each partner has a different family of origin, each has a different history. How the separate members of a couple move from being primarily the child of their parents to being primarily the partner of the spouse is complicated and slow.

Jack and Kathy Brett had been married for seven years when they entered therapy. They were a happy couple, pleased with their lives, their careers, and their beloved son, whom they described as a normal, playful three-year-old. They sat close to each other on my sofa, and were careful about each other's feelings as they described their situation.

Jack, a slight man, spoke first. His deep, resonant voice was surprising, coming from a person with so small a frame. I smiled to myself, realizing that I had imagined him as much larger when I had heard his voice on the telephone. He was a lawyer, successful in his work and important in his firm. He taught younger lawyers, was active in volunteer activities with the local bar association and his church. He was warm and intelligent. "We're going on vacation next week, and we always fight on vacation," he said, in a concerned tone. "I can't understand what happens to us when we're away. But I know I don't want it to happen again."

My mind started churning instantly. What was it about the forced intimacy of vacation time that this couple couldn't handle?

Kathy picked up the story. "We get there, and the tension rises. I can't make everyone happy, and I finally get really angry." Her voice, heavy with sadness, sounded frustrated and disappointed. "And we never have time to *talk,* so we never make it any better!" Kathy, a nurse who was staying home with Cody, their son, fiddled with the zipper on her parka lying next to her on the couch. Her large eyes went from Jack to me and back again, as if silently asking for a magical solution. I was confused—no time to talk on vacation with a three-year-old? Didn't the kid ever sleep?

"What usually happens on vacation?" I asked, and a riveting tale unfolded.

Jack and Kathy were both from a small town in the Midwest. They went home on every vacation, knowing that their parents missed seeing them and Cody. But when they arrived, neither set of parents could accommodate the family of three. Kathy's room at her parents' home was set up as it had been when she was in high school, with one twin bed. Jack's parents had turned his old bedroom into a study-den, with a pull-out couch; however, they had no additional place to put Cody. So the couple tried to accommodate to their surroundings and to their parents. Jack and Cody went to his parents' home; Kathy went to her parents' home. They met each day for meals, and spent their time shuttling Cody to Kathy's parents' home so that they could see him as much as Jack's parents did.

I was amazed and amused at their solution to the problem of sleeping arrangements. This couple had chosen to stay in their roles as children with each family of origin. Instead of establishing themselves as a marital unit, each functioned as a child "at home." They were never alone on vacation; they were always under the watchful eyes of one or both sets of parents. And when Cody needed to go to bed, each retired to the separate family home, to the childhood bed.

"How did this arrangement evolve?" I asked, curious about why they had chosen to spend their vacations in such a disrupted way. They appeared to be such a skilled couple, committed and connected. Why did they choose to be good children at the expense of their own time together?

The story was a sad one. The day before their wedding, soon after Jack passed the bar exam, Kathy's mother had discovered a lump in her breast. She told her husband, but no one told Jack and Kathy until they returned from their honeymoon, which was also a celebration of Jack's passing the bar, a three-week trip to Europe. By that time, Kathy's mother had had a radical mastectomy and was undergoing a powerful chemotherapy regimen.

Kathy was devastated. She felt guilty that she had been happy during the time her mother was so traumatized, and angry that she and Jack were kept in the dark about her mother's condition. She returned home to nurse her mother through the chemotherapy, using her considerable professional skills. Her mother and father, very grateful for her help, told her that she had made the difference between life and death.

After the crisis passed, Kathy returned to her new home with Jack. She was tearful and depressed, but managed to pick up her old job in the hospital. Both she and Jack returned frequently to their Midwest home to care for her mother. They stayed in their former homes, and that pattern had never changed.

Jack and Kathy, while successful marital partners and parents, had not been able to make a complete transition; they were still frozen in their old positions. They had not challenged their families to accept them as a couple, even though they felt loved and accepted by both sets of parents. Circumstances had prevented this couple from "cleaving" to each other, at least when they went "back home."

What must a couple do to establish themselves as a couple with their original families? Each person must begin to see the spouse as psychological home base, rather than turning primarily to parents. The couple must negotiate and agree about what information can and cannot be shared with the senior generation, when to have private time, when to share experiences with parents, how much contact to have, and when to have it. They must set up rules about privacy and intimacy, rules that are respectful of both parents and spouses, acknowledging the importance of both relationships in our lives. These adaptations must be made both between the spouses and with the parents. Some are explicit; others are not.

The Bretts' arrangement is a perfect case in point. There had never been any explicit discussion about their sleeping arrangements when they returned to their hometown. In fact, they were so used to it, and were surprised when I tried to talk about it. "It's only for a few nights," Jack said, "and it makes everyone happy to have time alone with their own child."

"Exactly," I replied, and watched the light of understanding switch on in Kathy's eyes.

"So you think it makes us crazy and angry at each other because we feel like children?" she asked. I nodded, and they looked at each other. Stared at each other for a long time. There was some communication going on between them, but I was unsure what it was. Finally, Kathy turned back to me and asked what they could do. They were very concerned about their parents' feelings, about how to make a change that was positive for everyone. But they were stuck in their old roles, which had only one solution, one that had failed them already.

By the end of our session, they had decided to sleep in a motel when they went home. They called their parents and told them that Cody would split the week between the two sets of grandparents, and that Jack and Kathy would visit with the families during the day. The solution worked perfectly.

What Jack and Kathy did was not just to create better sleeping arrangements for themselves; they established themselves as a married couple with their families. They made a change from "Jack" and "Kathy" to "Jack and Kathy." Both sets of parents were respectful of the change and enjoyed having Cody to themselves. Kathy's mother even asked, "What took you so long?"

In-law relationships are strange. These are people we have not chosen to be related to, but we will be involved with them—for better or worse—for the rest of our lives. These people will stay with our children, teach us about family tradition, drive us crazy, be intrusive or distant, and generally be around, whether or not we want them to be. For some people, these are relationships of support and intimacy; for others, they are the source of trouble and pain. They are relationships that are predicted by our popular culture to be among the most difficult of our lives. We expect—and are expected—to dislike our in-laws, to struggle with them.

Why Are In-Laws So Important?

What makes these relationships so emotionally loaded? Whether positive or negative, in-law associations are among the most intense in our lives. We see our in-laws as the source of problems in our spouses, as resources, as the topic of jokes. They are universally viewed through the lens of "mother-in-law" jokes, jokes that devalue the important and intimate connection between adults and the people who raised them. Our popular culture tells us that parents should not be too connected with their adult children, leaving that role to the spouse. Yet most of us love our parents, and many of us love the parents of our mates. How do some enjoy this intimate connection, even in defiance of our cultural mythology?

The transition to a healthy in-law relationship starts where you might expect—in a healthy relationship between parents and children. When children and parents genuinely like each other, it is much more likely that these positive feelings will spill over to a child's partner. But there is much more that must happen if the relationships are to work, and to work well.

First and foremost, there must be room for the new spouse in the family constellation. Families often expect a new spouse to adapt, much like a house guest, to the normal operations of the home. The new family member is welcome in the household, but is not expected to have any effect on the rest of the group, overtly or covertly. Obviously, this is neither a likely nor an optimal outcome. Each member of a family—new as well as old—should be expected to affect the family as a whole. Actually, the addition of a new family member changes the entire family constellation, because roles, and therefore rules, are realigned.

A friend of mine, Liza, married a man who became very ill on their honeymoon. He was rushed home from their vacation and immediately sent to the hospital, where for days he was evaluated by a medical team, while my friend and her new in-laws hovered at his bedside. Finally, the doctors came to the family to explain his condition. There were some difficult medical decisions to be made. Liza, a young newlywed, turned to her husband's parents and asked what they should do. To their credit, they refused to tell her. Her new mother-in-law said, "He is your husband now. You decide." They sat with her, listened to her dilemma, and surely influenced her decision. But at that critical moment, a new, respectful relationship was established between parents and new child. They showed her that they respected the sanctity of the new marriage and her pre-eminent place in her husband's life. They gracefully took a back seat and, probably without conscious thought, strengthened the new marriage and their own relationship with their daughter-in-law. In the days since, this couple has had issues between parents and children, but there is an assumption of respect and of position between them, an assumption that has carried them through difficult times.

My friend's new in-laws believed their son's marriage altered their place in his life, and they visibly demonstrated it during the critical hours in the hospital. They showed their daughter-in-law that they believed she was now his primary and most significant other, that the legal transition had produced an emotional transition as well. This is an important change, one that is verbalized—but not achieved—at the wedding ceremony. Most of us hope that our new mate—and his or her family—will make the huge psychological shift from "child of" to "spouse of" through the act of a marriage ceremony.

While this example is a dramatic one, our lives are replete with similar, simpler examples. Role changes can be positive or negative. I think it is helpful, however, to look at this isolated example and figure out what went right. Obviously, the parents recognized that they could influence the medical decisions about their son's care without having the final say. They knew their daughter-in-law would respect their ideas and concerns, as was evident in her asking them what should be done. She was respectful of their experience and advice, freely asking for their help. They saw her need for them and her fears, and also understood they could have an impact without diminishing her role in their son's life. In fact, her request also put them in a parental role toward her—she asked them to help much as she would have asked her own parents. Both parties saw they could make their difficult decisions together, rather than fighting over the ill husband and son; both parents and child-in-law acknowledged—and accepted—the importance of each other at this critical juncture in their lives together.

This scenario could have played out very differently. Had Liza not asked for help, or had her new in-laws taken over—and neither behavior would have been surprising—she might have felt disenfranchised with her new husband and his family. The parents might have taken over as parents, re-establishing themselves as the all-powerful decision-makers of his youth. Liza might have demanded that her in-laws absent themselves from the decision, forcing them to acknowledge her ultimate legal right to decide about her husband's life. In either case, the family would have been rocked by someone's insistence on being the most important person, rather than being part of a group of loving, concerned adults.

This point, while simple, was crucial to the successful outcome of this encounter. Liza and her in-laws allowed themselves to work cooperatively in pursuit of their joint goal. They were respectful of everyone's need to be involved. They acknowledged, through action, that they all loved the new husband and son, and that all of them, working together, were better able to create the best outcome. They acted as a family.

Family Roles

I imagine that the alternative scenario, had it played out, would have been due not to a desire to assert a personality but to solidify a position. In fact, most struggles with in-laws, especially early in marriage, are about position. We each know where we fit in our families, and Liza could have established her place in her husband's family by insisting on her pre-eminence. She would then have been erecting a boundary between herself and her husband's parents. In most cases, troubles with in-laws are less about who the people are in the family, and more about figuring out how they now fit together.

How we fit together is vitally important to people in families. Each of us has a role in our family of origin, a role that tells us what behavior is appropriate, how to talk, what to do, and what to expect others to do. A role is a script for behavior, allowing us to know how we fit in the family. It teaches us our proper place in our earliest relationships. Each of us operates according to a script, and most of us are totally unaware of it!

EXERCISE 18: Try to figure out some of the rules and roles from your original family. Remember your adolescence. Did you or a sibling get away with misbehavior? What was the explanation given to the other children? Was that child the baby, the rebel, or the favored one? Which of your parents was the disciplinarian? Who had more overt power in the day-to-day running of the household? Who had more covert power? All of these are examples of family roles, the accepted organizational chart of the family.

These rules, this unspoken organization, help individuals in the family know what their roles and behaviors should be. We understand *how* relationships work. We learn who can talk to whom in what way, who is allowed to bend the rules, who must stay within the letter of the law. These rules are critically important to the smooth running of the family, so important that the family may not be able to brook behavior that is inconsistent with the unstated code. For example, a family where the mother has been a competent professional may find it difficult to integrate her inability to cope with a colicky baby. She has always been able to do anything! Why is she having so much trouble with a small infant?

We work not only under family rules; we operate under the influence of society's rules as well. The nineteenth-century couplet goes: "Oh my son's a son till he gets him a wife, but my daughter's my daughter all her life" (which I believe to be untrue). It tells us that we should expect men to become separate from their parents on marriage, while women stay in intimate relationships with their original families forever. If this is true, imagine the loss for both parents and son as these important connections are suddenly severed. Mothers and fathers lose their sons. Sons lose their parents. How can we be surprised when some parents resist the interloper who has stolen their child—regardless of whether or not they like her!

An interesting part of this adaptation is in the area of terms of address. Most of us struggle with what we should call our in-laws. The man and woman, though not our parents, may expect to be called Mom and Dad. Many of us are uncomfortable using these titles for people we know very little or not at all. What should we call them, and who decides? Do you call your in-laws by their first names, or Mom and Dad, or simply avoid using names for them altogether? In some families, this issue is very important, as mothers, fathers, daughters, and sons all have definite ideas about the appropriate names for their new relations. Again, the name chosen may be part of the rules of the relationship. A person you call by her first name is very different from a person you call Mom.

In or Out?

How do families accept or reject a new family member? How does the behavior of the new "child" affect his or her place in the extended family?

EXERCISE 19: Recall what you were first told about the members of your partner's family. How were they described to you? What impressions did you have of them——even before meeting them? Make a list of your early reactions, then consider how——and why——your impressions have evolved.

Obviously, there are many aspects to the inclusion of a new person in the family constellation. In some sense, we are all scripted into our relationships with our new in-laws. Society tells us that we may find them intrusive, or that we may expect a great deal from them. Our own mate tells us how we are to experience this new family, by presenting them as positive or negative, as competitors or cooperators, approving or disapproving. Imagine, for example, that your mate has told you he dislikes or distrusts his parents. Most of us would assume that our partner's perceptions are valid and correct, and would adopt an untrusting attitude, without evaluating them on our own. We assume that our loved one's beliefs about the world——or at least this part of the world——are generally correct, and we may take them as our own. If we expect to like or dislike our new in-laws, chances are good that we will find aspects of their behavior that confirm this belief.

We also learn whether we are more or less important than our partner's parents——and in what circumstances. Obviously, there are circumstances where the needs of our original family impinge on the needs of our mate: in extreme illness, death, or other crises. How each of us evaluates the relative importance of these needs is different and, frankly, instinctive. Some of us may crave greater separateness and privacy, while others want to remain in the thick of the original family. We all use our inner barometer to measure the acceptability of the different expectations of closeness and distance——often in ways that upset our partners!

EXERCISE 20: What is your relationship with your family? Are you close? Distant? Argumentative? Do you enjoy each other? How do you expect your partner's relationship with your family to be similar to or different from yours? From your relationship with your partner's family?

For some couples, a new family member may actually make the original relationships closer. A distant man, for example, may marry a woman who is better able to talk to his family, who may increase the intimacy between him and his parents. We often marry people with skills different from our own, so it is not surprising for an individual to pick a partner who is better able to be close or better able to be more distant than ourselves.

Marital Choice

How does this happen? We all choose our mates to "improve" ourselves, picking partners we perceive to have different skills. These different abilities are generally in areas where we fear ourselves are wanting. A man may pick a woman who can bring him closer to his family, because she has better interpersonal skills. She may pick him to allow her greater distance in her intimate relationships, as she feels overwhelmed by such relationships. A woman may pick a partner who will impress her parents, who have hurt her by not adequately admiring her accomplishments. It is typical for us to choose partners who will help us negotiate the world and our intimate relationships. Not surprisingly, we are later amazed when our marriage grows to maturity and these aspects of our marital choice give us trouble.

The process is simple, though often surprising. We pick our mates for many characteristics, from reliability to sexual attractiveness. These aspects of marital choice are very personal, varying from person to person. One aspect of marital choice, however, may be described as "anything but . . ." It concerns the personality characteristics we try to avoid in a mate. We look for a partner who is unlike our families in important attitudes. For example, a man may find a wife who seems more emotionally available than his mother, or enjoys sporting activities more than his mother, or is more intellectual than his father. The attributes are appealing on their own and also exemplify an unconscious choice away from some unsatisfying aspect of the parent-child relationship. The partner is chosen not only for her own appeal—and the positive ways she reminds of us our original intimate relationships—but also for her differences from these original relationships.

This seems a sensible approach to marital choice. It helps us better ourselves, both by allowing us to continue the parts of our intimate relations we enjoy, and by providing us the opportunity to change the aspects we are uncomfortable with. Selecting our partner is an opportunity for us to change the behaviors and patterns we learned in our original family, simply because the partner expects different behaviors, based on a different family history. Problems arise, however, when we begin to search for those behaviors we have come to expect from intimate relationships, patterns of behavior that were set down in our original family.

In Chapter 4, we looked at birthday behaviors from our childhoods. These behaviors form a standard against which we evaluate future birthdays, in terms of what we liked and what we disliked. We have similar standards for almost all behaviors, from birthdays to marital fighting, to forms and levels of intimacy. We may pick a partner who has different expectations for our behavior, but this will not necessarily change our standards, our expectations, or our behavior at all! In fact, there are couples who, in choosing each other, know that they will have to compromise and adapt to each other's background—and who proceed to spend much of their time debating, discussing, and quarreling about how to make the partner over into the family each came from!

Coral and Doug Lopatti came into therapy to deal with Coral's problems with Doug's parents. She was a dance teacher who worked nights at a local dance studio. He was an electrician who worked in his family's business. They were newly married, and she was already furious at his entire family. The couple came to therapy after Coral broke down in tears in her doctor's office. She had hurt her ankle, and when the doctor told her to stay off her foot for a week, she cried and cried. He sent the couple to me.

Coral hobbled in. She was strikingly beautiful. Her long brown hair tumbled down her back and framed a lovely face. As far as I could tell, she wore no makeup. Her husband was no less attractive and fit. They were an exquisite pair.

Coral began to talk. "When Dr. Cohen said I had to stay home, all I could think about was Doug's parents. How they would come over and bother me. How they would tell me to quit my job. How they would criticize me and tell me I'm a lousy wife. They think my job is unimportant. No, they think my job is bad! They think that only a cheap woman would go dancing with strange men!"

"Oh, come on. You're overreacting," Doug interjected.

"I am not. You don't hear them. You don't see them. You think they're great."

"They're my parents."

"And your employers. And they don't pay you enough to live on. How can I stop working? We can't live on your salary!"

"Oh, yeah. Like you'd really stop working anyhow."

"Well, maybe I would."

The discussion was going nowhere fast. Both Doug and Coral were flinging accusations, unable or unwilling to stay focused. I tried to bring them back to the present. "What's the real problem?"

"His parents. They drive me crazy!"

I responded slowly, wondering whether Coral could accept what I was about to say. "His parents are out of your control. In some sense, you're simply stuck with them. Given that, what's the problem?"

Doug nodded. "I can't change them either. I wish she'd stop trying to make them different." Had he removed himself from the problem altogether? Could he be involved in a solution?

Coral's voice rose. "I wish *you'd* be different with them—or quit the damn job!" This was a new complaint—not about Doug's parents but about his relationship with them. Doug had already taken a position on this issue, however: he said he couldn't do anything. I knew he was surprised that his passivity had not calmed his wife. Instead, it was enraging her!

Coral's anger was not surprising. In fact, I wondered if it was the behavior Doug needed from her. Doug had a problem he couldn't solve—his impotence with his parents. He was a child in this important relationship, unable to garner his parents' respect for his wife or his work abilities. It made sense that this made him angry. But he seemed unable to express his own discomfort with the elder Lopattis. Maybe Doug had chosen Coral to help him deal with his parents.

To help him deal with his parents? How? It would be quite simple. Doug admitted that he saw his relationship with his parents as a trouble spot, but chose to stay passive. I knew he complained to Coral about them, even though he refused to help solve the problem. Coral, correctly but unconsciously perceiving that her husband needed help in changing this important relationship, took over the job. Suddenly the problem with Doug's parents became Coral's problem. She felt that they were unfair, judgmental, and unkind. Doug could sit back and watch her get upset, and then he could defend them.

In fact, Doug was experiencing his anger toward his parents by watching Coral express his feelings for him. Couples and individuals do this all the time. It is much the same experience as going to a sad movie when you want to cry, or watching an adventure or fight film when you're angry. We are capable of feeling through the experiences of others. Having vicarious feelings may, in fact, be an easier way to feel, because it is more distant and less powerful. When couples have tape-recorded fights, I always ask myself, "Whose feelings are these? Who needs to say or feel these emotions?" We can easily teach our mates to express our emotions for us. All of us do it all the time.

Doug had transferred to Coral his resentment toward the elder Lopattis. Instead of expressing it himself, he had told his wife that his parents were intrusive and unfair. She believed him and repeated his thoughts back to him; then he denied them. So Coral was left to be angry at her in-laws, which allowed Doug to maintain a more cordial, working relationship with them.

This unconscious act of splitting up our feelings so that each partner can express only one point of view has two effects. First, Coral could not see the Lopattis as anything but malevolent and unfair. She resented the time the families spent together. Second, Doug could continue to see them as loving and involved parents, on his side—largely because Coral was expressing all of their joint hostility. Her anger was a combination of Doug's and her own.

What Happens with In-Laws?

Relations with a new family—and with its unspoken rules—are necessarily complicated. Each member of the couple must not only negotiate a relationship with the new in-laws, but must also negotiate a new relationship with the original family as they find room for the new spouse in the old family constellation. How we do this depends on many factors, including our unconscious intentions. If (and this is usually the case) we pick our partners to expand our own repertoire of behaviors, then it should be no surprise that we choose someone who is different from ourselves—and from our families. This will necessarily create tension, as the old family tries to integrate a new member, one who may not behave according to family rules at all!

Cinderella and her prince, for example, have radically different backgrounds. He is indulged and loved. His courtiers will meet his every need, even to the extent of inviting all the girls in the kingdom to a ball so that he can choose amongst them. At no point is there even a consideration that a girl might not want to marry the prince. He is every maiden's fantasy. We imagine him as handsome and kind.

Cinderella, in contrast, was abandoned and is unloved. Her parents are dead, leaving her to the whims of an abusive, depriving stepmother. She is often unfed. Her clothes are in tatters. Her stepmother thinks so little of her that she's not even concerned about leaving Cinderella home on the night of the ball; the stepdaughter is not a person, so there's no thought that she would attend.

Imagine what happens when these two try to integrate, not only with each other, but with their original families. What will the king think of this ragamuffin his son is married to? Can she be expected to understand the way her new family works? She is used to being unloved—how will she respond when her new husband chooses to attend to affairs of state rather than to her needs? What will happen when her new father-in-law gets angry at her for something she didn't understand was wrong? We do not even have to turn to fairy tales: Diana Spencer—Princess Di—seems to have suffered from these woes, and she was hardly an orphaned ragamuffin.

Given the radical differences in the backgrounds of this fantasy couple, it should come as no surprise that they might not live "happily ever after." It is also reasonable that their problems will not be confined to those of communication, that the very existence of their separate families will create tension and discomfort. His father will surely want to take over, controlling and teaching her to become a princess, worthy of Prince Charming. Her stepmother will intrude and demand access to all that she has—the castle, the courtiers, the money. The way in which the newlywed couple negotiates the demands of each family will determine each family's place in the couple's world.

The Importance of Mom and Dad

For the extended family will certainly remain in the couple's world. Our relationship with our parents is an ongoing, permanent part of our lives. Parents, whether dead or alive, near or distant, loved or reviled, are fundamental pieces of our psychological makeup. We do not completely move outside our parents' influence, no matter what our wishes may be. We are closely connected to these people—for better or for worse—even past the demarcation "till death do us part." Relationships between parents and adult children are critically important to all members of the family. In fact, one of the great illusions of modern time is that we can actually sever these intense bonds. In reality, the attachment between parent and child is passionate and is essential to both. We may move away from our original families, both physically and psychologically, but we are never away from their influence and importance. So basic is the original family that many therapists are much more interested in childhood issues than in present-day problems!

Simply put, we cannot divorce our parents. This connection influences and shapes our adult patterns and behaviors, our expectations and hopes. While each of us can make changes in these patterns and hopes, the relationship between parents and children makes an indelible impression on our adult psyche.

If we cannot divorce our parents, then we should not have to choose between parents and spouse. Although this makes obvious sense, the experience of many adults is the exact opposite. Many people feel that their parents or in-laws place an intolerable burden on their relations with their partner.

Sometimes the hardship is quite clear—when parents actively dislike their child's choice of mate—but more often it is subtle. The new in-laws, whether parents or children, may object to the behaviors or beliefs of their new family members. They may place their loved one in the position of having to choose—in effect asking, "Whom do you love more?"

In fact, the most likely way to divorce our in-laws is to divorce our spouse. There are many instances where this is the ultimate outcome of the in-law struggle: the marriage of the children does not survive the tension between parents and children related only through marriage.

This is, of course, an outcome to be avoided. It is essential that in-laws, both parents and children, do not put their shared family member—the child of the parents, the spouse of the adult child—in the position where he or she must choose in which relationship to remain.

How can we achieve this? On the surface, the rules are simple, although they may be difficult to carry out. We need to continue to work at these relationships, often for the duration of our marriage.

Making In-Law Relationships Work

Each of us should understand that our relations with our in-laws are a permanent, important part of the marital landscape. We need to be respectful and act appropriately, incorporating these people into our lives. To do so, we have to establish the basic components of the relationship.

- First and foremost, recognize that your spouse is in a permanent relationship with his or her parents. Effectively, this means that each of us must be especially careful to maintain at least a cordial relationship with our in-laws. For, while you may not like these people, you are related to them. Treat them accordingly. They are members of your clan, no matter what you think of them!

• Work hard to understand how your mate's family works. What are the unspoken rules? How do people get their needs met? Make the assumption that they do *not* operate in the same way your family does. Do not try to make them into your family, but try to find your own place in their family. Adapt to each other—*SLOWLY!*

• Your in-laws are not *your* family. They should not be witness to your most uninhibited self. Understand that if you show these people your worst or most casual behavior, they may think badly of you. Do not behave with them any differently from the way you would with other acquaintances, especially early in your relationship. Do not fight in front of them, show them your worst table manners, or tell them the most lurid stories of your past!

• Understand your expectations. What you want this relationship to be will influence your perceptions of what it actually is.

• Establish your own relationship with your new family. Do not hide behind your child or spouse. Learn to speak directly—and respectfully—to your in-laws. Talk for yourself.

• Understand that this is a long-term relationship. It will change over time. Do not feel the need to make it perfect right now, but realize that you—and your in-laws—have lots of time to make mistakes *and* make amends.

- Apologize when you hurt other people, even when it seems silly to you.

- Establish limits of privacy, for yourself and with your spouse, so that you know what is open to discussion and what is not. Do not drop in, unless you are invited to do so. Do not expect in-laws to drop in. Do not expect to be at every family gathering of both families, but be flexible.

- Try, as much as possible, to integrate both extended families. They are all involved in the life of your new family, the family of you and your spouse.

- No matter how disappointing the relationship may be, keep trying to improve it. Don't quit, and don't reciprocate in kind—unless it's good stuff! You may be in this relationship for the rest of your life. Always look and work toward improvement, and try to be optimistic!

SUGGESTIONS FOR FURTHER THOUGHT

- What do you call your in-laws? What do they want to be called? Why?

- How do you show respect to your in-laws? When is it appropriate to disagree?

- Who talks about "hot" topics with your in-laws? What topics are off-limits? Who decides?

- Consider your feelings for your in-laws. Do they know how you feel about them? How do you want the relationship to progress? What are you doing to get on that path?

Money is one of the thorniest
issues the new couple will face. Prince Charming
has lots of money and all the privilege that money
brings. Cinderella has been poor for a long time, and has
created a life that values singing over money. When they
marry, will he feel that the kingdom's money is his or
theirs? Will she feel entitled to spend the money?
Will he learn to respect what she values? How
will they change each other?

7

MONEY

THE STERNS WALKED INTO MY OFFICE FOR A
first session. Frannie, a large, loud woman, had made the
appointment. She called at the recommendation of her
gynecologist after a tearful doctor's visit; she had
complained to Dr. Smith that she was very unhappy but was
unsure why. The gynecologist phoned me before the session—a
rare occurrence. Dr. Smith was concerned about the Sterns, and
wondered whether Frannie needed to see a psychiatrist for
antidepressant medication. I could hear the worry in his voice.

Frannie was big—much taller than my five foot three inches.
She was hugely pregnant—which surprised me. Neither Dr.
Smith nor Frannie had told me that she was near delivery. I felt

dwarfed by her physical presence. She waddled past me to the couch and sat down with a huge exhalation of breath. Her husband, John, followed. He was tall and equally imposing. He was well dressed and had presence. I wondered—as I always do—what John's job was. This is a silly game I play with new patients. I imagine what they do in their work life; it amazes me how often I am correct. I suppose that we really do wear the uniform of our job.

John looked like an investment banker. His suit was expensive, his shoes immaculate. Frannie was harder to read. Her pregnancy distracted me from my game, but I guessed her to be a teacher. I wasn't sure. I glanced at her large hands, and decided she was an artist. Her nails were chipped and irregular. Those were hands that worked hard.

The game takes only seconds. We began the session. "What brings you here today?"

"The baby," started Frannie. "I'm worried about the baby." I waited, not sure where we were going. There was a pause, and then John took over from his wife. "This is our first child. Frannie is worried that the baby isn't all right."

"And that I won't be a good mother. That's important, too. I don't know anything about babies." She looked at her husband as if she needed help. He stared at me. I was still confused. Most new parents are worried about their ability to parent. What else was going on here? What made Dr. Smith concerned enough to call me? Or even to consider medication for a pregnant woman?

We sat together for an hour, talking about the pregnancy and their anticipation of the baby's birth. We talked about their jobs, John's as a successful banker; Frannie's as a designer for a contemporary furniture company. They told funny stories about their families' reactions to the pregnancy. Throughout, I was aware of Frannie's sorrow and John's attempts to cheer her up. The entire session seemed to me incomplete and confusing. I was aware that something going on was not being discussed. On the surface, the Sterns talked about real issues, but they never let me in. I wondered whether I could help them.

As we wound up the session, I gave them some feedback on the problems, normalizing Frannie's concern, trying to draw John in to support her. Then we talked about the process of therapy, and finally we came to the practical issues of scheduling and fees. After setting another appointment, John turned to Frannie. "Whose is this?" he asked.

"I don't know. I guess it's mine. What do you think?" She turned to me for my opinion. I had no idea what the question meant.

"About what? Is there a problem with the appointment?"

"No, no. That's fine." I was still confused. What were they asking? After waiting a moment for my response, Frannie asked impatiently, "Who should pay for this?"

"Is there an issue with the insurance company?" I was completely baffled.

"No." I could hear the irritation in John's voice. "Which one of us should pay you?"

Suddenly, I understood. The Sterns kept their money separate, and they wanted me to decide which of them should pay for their joint therapy! I asked them to hold the discussion until the next session, in deference to the time. One week later, we met again. After exchanging greetings and hearing about their week, I asked them to tell me about their money arrangements.

John took the lead. "Well, I'm a banker. I like to invest money, and sometimes I invest in risky ventures. Frannie is more cautious, so she keeps her income separate from mine. That way we always have money for the mortgage."

"So your money pays for the household expenses, Frannie, and yours is for your investments, John?"

"Yes," Frannie answered slowly. I could hear her discomfort. "But I don't know what will happen now."

"I don't see what the issue is, Frannie," John retorted. "Why should anything change?"

"Because of the baby. Whose responsibility is the baby?" John stared at Frannie. It was clear he really did not understand what she was asking him. I suggested that she be more explicit. She seemed very uncomfortable, but she pressed on. "John, I'm not sure that I can pay for all of the baby's stuff on my salary. I think we may have to use some of your money."

"My money? Why? How much can one little baby cost?" John's surprise was evident—and humorous. He was almost outraged. He looked at his wife with shock. "Why should anything change?" he asked for the second time.

Many of us think of money as simply a form of exchange. We earn money for working, and we spend money for things we want and need. We work to pay for our housing, our food, our vacations. Our jobs may be fun and interesting, but they also give us the funds to obtain those things we feel we need. Some of us would work without pay, but very few. Money is one of the ways a society shows that it values the work and achievements of its members, and it is also power.

Power

It is easy for us to understand that money and power are related. People with more money have greater options in the world, are able to influence others, to spend their time with greater freedom, to fund the organizations they find compelling. Money helps elect public officials, educate children according to personal or societal values, and pay for household help. Money allows us to lead our lives with more choices. But money is not only powerful in a couple's interactions with the external world; it has a potent effect within the couple, too.

For the Sterns, money had multiple meanings. Frannie's

money was joint money, used to pay for their lives together. She paid for the mortgage, the utilities, and the food. Her money supported the family. John's money was his, used to fund his interests. I wondered how this arrangement had come to be, and how each member of the couple felt about it now.

"Explain this to me," I asked. "How is money divided? How did you make this deal?" For it surely was a deal between the Sterns. Maybe not a fair deal, but a deal nonetheless.

John answered. "Well, Frannie used to make a lot more money than I did, when I was in training and just starting out in the business. She had the money to pay the big bills, and I paid the smaller ones, like the phone bill and the electric bill. But as she made more money, she started paying the smaller ones too. It just made sense to have one person writing the checks. When I started making money, well, then, we decided to save my money." I noticed that he referred to his income as *my* money. "But I kept making more money. Suddenly I was making more than Frannie, so I started playing with some of it. I'm good at investing, so I used my money to make more money. It made sense."

"Does it still make sense?" I asked them both.

"Why not?" John looked at me as if I were absurd. "What's changed?" Frannie, who had been silent during his explanation of their financial arrangements, looked at him. I asked her what she was thinking.

"But, John, you make so much more money, don't you?"

Alarm bells went off in my head. "Do you know how much money John earns, Frannie?" I asked.

"Well, I work on commission, so it varies," John answered for Frannie.

"But do you know, Frannie?" She didn't answer; she was looking at her hands. I turned to John. "How much do you make?"

The question always surprises people. In our society, no one asks how much people earn. That secret is kept more closely than our sex lives or our traumatic childhoods. We are more likely to know whether our friends have had abortions than how much they earn. But it is important information between any couple. We need to know how much money we make, and how it gets spent.

> EXERCISE 21: How much money do you and your spouse earn? Who pays the bills? How much do you have in savings? Who does the taxes? How much money is available for nonessential expenditures, such as vacations, electronic gadgets, hobbies, expensive clothing, entertainment? How do you decide what is essential and what is nonessential? Who decides?

Couples are often surprised when I begin to put emphasis on these issues. I am often astonished at how many couples have not exchanged essential information about their financial standing. It is quite common for one person to be in control of the couple's finances; the other partner often is ignorant about money.

Ignorance about money is more than a lack of knowledge. It rapidly leads to an imbalance of power. The partner who is financially responsible makes decisions about the couple's future, about vacations, about housing—the full range of the family's activities—without the full input of both parties. Inevitably, one person is left to feel out of control of the decision-making process. If I, for example, do not know how much money my husband earns, how can I decide how I should spend money? How can I make vacation plans, or even plans to attend a professional conference? How can I decide where to shop for food, for clothing, for his birthday presents? Of course, many of these decisions are made together, but many are made independently. I need to form my own opinions, and for that, I require information. Money knowledge gives me the power to act on my own.

When one partner is out of the loop of financial knowledge,

there is a disparity of power and responsibility. Frannie had no idea how much money John made, how much he lost in the stock market, or where any of his money was at any given time. How could she be a full partner in the marriage?

I believe that the ways we discuss money and its attendant issues are of paramount importance in any marriage. Whether we have too little money or just enough (we so rarely feel that we have too much!), all of us have strong emotional responses to money, savings, and expenditures. We care about how much we are paid, and are offended when an expected raise does not appear. We have strong opinions on how money is used, whether it is saved, invested, or spent indulgently. In fact, one person's extravagance is another's essential expenditure. When these differences exist, they can have severe consequences within a marriage.

The Sterns did not have equal access to information about their financial status. John knew what Frannie made as a designer for the furniture company, but she had no idea how much he earned. She had no idea how much money he was making—or losing—through his investments. Indeed, she had no idea what these investments were. For all she knew, John had bought some stocks that were soaring—and she could quit her job when the baby was born if she so chose. Or maybe he was losing his entire salary every year. She needed to know, but John wanted to keep the information close to the vest. Lack of communication about this critical subject is frequent. But it can create such serious problems that I almost always pursue—and try to destabilize— this arrangement. I know it can be a hot issue, so I go slowly, but there wasn't a lot of time before the Sterns' baby would be born.

"John, do you know what you make?"

"Of course I do. And so could Frannie if she looked at our tax returns." He was putting the responsibility for her lack of knowledge in Frannie's corner. I decided not to pursue this side issue, and returned to the topic of money.

"So you have no objection to her seeing your tax forms? You file jointly?"

"No. I mean, she can see whatever she wants, but we file separately. Seems simpler."

Frannie jumped in, leaning toward John. "Then just tell me. What's the problem with telling me?"

John looked at his wife and sat back in his chair. Her anxiety seemed to soften him. He was in charge now. I noticed that her intervention into my conversation with him seemed to relax him, as though the tension had been diminished. She had taken him off the hot seat with me, back into a comfortable, repeated discussion with her. I decided to jump back in.

"John, do you know how much money you earned last year?"

"In general. I know what my base salary was and how much commission I made. I have a general idea how much I made in the stock market, too. But I don't have the exact numbers."

"Frannie, do you want to know now? John has just said that he has some information in his head." I was unsure whether she would insist on learning her husband's salary. Many women protect their partners by avoiding factual information, preferring to know a general salary range, or even nothing, if the woman perceives that her husband needs to keep this a secret. If Frannie didn't want the knowledge now, it would mean that there was more exploration to be done before we tackled the details about money. But she pursued it.

"Yes, I want to know. John, I want to know now." She sounded tougher, more insistent. She sat forward in her seat, her large belly protruding. Her hands stroked her abdomen, holding the baby. She was imposing, different from how she had appeared only a few minutes before. John reacted to her stronger stance as he had earlier, but with less conviction.

"What's the big deal? You never needed to know before."

"I need to know now. I need to know because of the baby. It's not just you and me now." Frannie was explaining why the rules had changed for her so that John could understand and adapt. "I need to know what we have for this child, and I need to know for me, so that I can make decisions." John stared at his hands, avoiding his wife's gaze.

Money and Gender

Money often represents different issues for men and women. Women tend to see it as a means to an end. Money is how we pay for what we want, whether it is food or vacations or college for the children. Money is purposeful, and its meaning is mostly about what it can bring to the couple.

Men tend to see money in much more complicated ways. Of course, money is a means to an end, but it is also an external evaluation of a person's worth. Not just his or her financial worth, but inherent worth. Men and women are both emotionally invested in their salaries, but men tend to see their income as an objective assessment of their value *as a person*. This perception can lead a man to feel that money is not only an estimate of what he's worth, but also of what he's *not* worth. Thus, a man's income information may be very hard for him to share with others. For many men, telling their actual income feels like getting naked in front of a group of strangers. It can feel humiliating and uncomfortable, and disclosing such personal information can make them feel they've given others power over them.

This gender difference may lessen as women enter the higher ranks of the workforce, but I see no evidence that it is disappearing. Women seem to get more sense of self-worth from areas of their lives other than income, while men still seem trapped by this external—and limited—measurement. Most of the couples I see seem to understand this difference at an unconscious level. In fact, it is common for wives to try to protect their husbands from divulging this important assessment of their worth, as they sense the multiple meanings of money.

The biggest question for me is not what people make, but how they feel about what they earn. I wondered why John felt such a powerful need to keep his income a secret. Did it disguise some hidden shame about his compensation? Although this is not uncommon, I thought John's impulse was different. I believed that he just didn't want to tell Frannie—and that this particular issue served an important function in their marriage. They were struggling about money to avoid struggling about something else.

Money struggles—like most ongoing marital struggles— generally mask other issues. In fact, decisions about money, expenditures, and saving can be easily made when they are actually about the nuts and bolts of finances, open and above board. I am often impressed by the innovative ways couples divide money responsibilities. Many of these divisions are healthy for the couple, and presume the marriage will last. Others surprise me with their pessimism.

Prenuptial Agreements and Other Arrangements

I am not a lawyer, so I do not advise couples on the legalities of prenuptial agreements. As a therapist, however, I view these legal documents as predivorce settlements. They are filled with pessimism, assuming the possibility of the worst outcome. I wonder whether the couple that has such an agreement comes to the marriage with the optimism and hopefulness that are essential for marriage. I understand that the legal agreement may protect assets in the long run (and may have a particularly legitimate function where families from prior marriages or family assets are involved), but I confess that it makes me uncomfortable.

I also wonder about the couple's future when all monies are kept separate. Often, these people each allocate a percentage toward joint expenses, keeping in mind some artificial sense of what's fair. Again, this implies a lack of trust in both the partner and the relationship, and it makes the financial aspects of the relationship too important—all the time. The couple divides up dinner checks, groceries, utilities, and rent. The financial arrangements are complex and important. The transaction often shows great creativity, but also demonstrates a pronounced sense of separateness between the partners. I am concerned about the impact such money dealings have on the relationship as a whole.

My problem with both of these arrangements is simple. I believe that marriage is a partnership—a partnership of goals, emotions, problems, and assets. I cannot imagine being in a marital relationship with widely disparate, maybe even unknown goals. I cannot imagine withholding important information from my husband. Not surprisingly, our money is jointly held. While we both acknowledge that his income is higher than mine, we also understand that my other contributions to our family's life have value above and beyond the monetary. He may bring in more dollars than I do, but the money belongs to both of us, reflecting our jointly held belief that each of us brings more than income to our family.

There are many ways a couple can develop good financial patterns. In some couples, one partner is more fiscally competent, so that spouse may be the one who pays bills and balances the checkbook. In others, each partner may maintain a separate account, but the information about both accounts is shared openly and without coercion. Money is a topic of conversation, not an area of conflict. The couple may or may not share basic values about their financial life, but they are respectful of each other's needs and views. One may want to spend while the other wants to save, but they work out a mutually acceptable solution—one that involves spending and saving!

The Sterns were far from this point. Frannie clearly felt that she was powerless to influence John's financial dealings. John felt that he was acting in the best interests of his growing family, and was hurt by his wife's distrust. He could not understand why she continued to "demand" information. Did it mean that she thought he was irresponsible? He was unlikely to tell her what she wanted to know, because he inferred only a question about his competence.

There were lots of ways to move at this point. I could bully John into revealing his income, or explore money's meaning to each member of the couple, for we all have intense feelings about money. The emotional responses come from the family of origin, our present perceptions of our worth, and the climate in the marriage. As important a symbol and tool of power as money is, it is more; it symbolizes security, autonomy, and nurturance as well.

Money as Security

For John Stern, money represented his need for security. He felt a greater sense of control—over his future and his wife—when he had sole say over their joint expenditures. He was able to determine how and when their money was spent and saved. This control made him feel that Frannie was dependent on him, and therefore more securely tied to him. In fact, his strategy was having the opposite effect. Frannie was angry with John's need for control and resentful of his autocratic ways. But John found that his ability to dictate the financial dealings of the family made him feel safer in the marriage.

Money can represent security in other ways, too. Obviously, a couple with savings has greater fiscal security; they are less likely to lose their house or other possessions. But money also has emotional worth. It can make people feel safe in their relationship and in the world. We may feel stronger, more capable, more powerful, feelings that help create a sense of security.

Money as Nurturance

Many couples are surprised when one partner sees money as the ultimate nurturer. This spouse needs to have money, to spend money. He or she buys and saves to create the sense of being cared for. I see this often in my office, where one member of the couple spends wildly on himself or herself, in an almost frantic attempt to "fill oneself." The purchases are often irrelevant; the spending is all that counts.

Money can also represent nurturance is less pathological ways. Most of us, for example, expect to be remembered on our birthday—with a present. A birthday card may feel totally inadequate, demonstrating that it's *not* the thought that counts—it's the gift. And we may judge the quality of the gift on many variables, including how much it cost. We may measure how much the other person cares based on the time, effort, and expense that went into the present. Thus, the ways we spend are often translated into the ways we feel.

Frannie Stern saw money as nurturance. She believed that she was caring for John by taking care of the household bills. She even felt that this "nurturance" excused her from the obligation of other caretaking. She was not very involved in his daily life, in listening to his stories of success and frustration, in sharing the details of each day. While both members of the couple explained this away because he worked evenings, John was unhappy about the distance. He described himself as lonely. Later, John would complain that paying bills was one of very few nurturing actions Frannie ever made toward him. She paid the mortgage but didn't kiss him good night. Frannie was surprised that John felt the need for anything more.

Money as Autonomy

Money gives us freedom. The ability to spend and save allows each of us to experience ourselves as capable of taking care of our own needs. For some people, this autonomy is essential to their sense of well-being. They need to know that they have the freedom to make independent decisions, or even to leave the relationship, without enormous financial consequences. For these people, money may simply represent independence.

John Stern also had this perception of money. He believed that Frannie was more likely to leave the relationship if she had the autonomy that money brought. His fears about his wife's reliability kept him from opening up about his income and investments.

> EXERCISE 22: What did money mean in your family of origin? What was the attitude toward spending and saving? Who had control over the money? Who wanted the control? Did people tell the truth about their spending habits?
>
> What does money mean to you in your current relationship? Do you rely on your income to provide safety, caring, power, control, independence? Who makes more money? Does it matter? Is your money jointly held? Are you satisfied with your financial arrangements?

For the Sterns, money had all of these meanings. Money was a way to communicate nurturing, control, independence, and safety. Even though they both thought they had agreed to a system, their arrangement was failing them. We had to develop new rules.

After much soul-searching, John decided to tell Frannie his

income. He brought his tax returns into my office and went over them with his wife. Suddenly, the superficial nature of their interactions changed. John was able to tell Frannie his fears about the coming child, and she confessed her strong urge to continue working. They decided that she should try to negotiate part-time work, which she was able to do.

The Sterns were on their way to resolving the original problem. They had identified what each was concerned about, and had begun to search for solutions. Each partner was willing to share more with the other, exposing previously secret worries. They talked about money and its meaning in their relationship, and stopped using it to mask other issues. They began to communicate.

SUGGESTIONS FOR FURTHER THOUGHT

- Look at the patterns of spending and saving that you brought from your original family. How do you still follow these patterns? Do they work for you now?

- Who controls the finances in your marriage? How did this come about?

- How did your parents' financial relationship affect their marriage? Was there resentment or agreement about the meaning of money? How does your financial relationship affect your marriage?

- Think about money differences as a gender issue. Does it apply to your relationship?

- Do you have a budget or an agreed-upon financial plan? Have you tried to make one?

- What is essential and what are luxuries? If you have different ideas about what is essential and what is not, how do you decide what to buy?

- What financial goals do you share? How are you pursuing these goals?
- If you suddenly acquired a windfall of money, how would you use it? To pay bills, to go on a vacation, as savings?

The prince and Cinderella have their first fight. They yell and scream at each other. Each feels misunderstood, hurt. Even after they calm down and make up, the bad feelings remain. They decide not to fight again—it's too scary. But what should they do the next time they disagree?

8

FIGHTING

E VERY COUPLE FIGHTS. OFTEN ONE OF THE GREAT shocks—and one of the great disappointments—of early marriage is arguing. Whether a couple calls it an argument, disagreement, quarrel, discussion, or fight, a debate about needs and expectations can get heated and intense, disturbing and upsetting. Usually the topic of the quarrel seems silly or mean, at least in retrospect. Often couples complain that their fights make no sense to them.

Fred and Sally Parke had been married less than a year when they came to therapy. The fight that precipitated the call to me had been about a relatively trivial issue, and neither was concerned about the original topic. During the course of their heated argument, however, Fred had got up and started to pace their small living room. Sally was frightened, and she tried to control her anxiety. Then Fred yelled something—neither could remember exactly what—and came closer to her. She panicked and ran to her car. The Parkes spoke on the phone the day after, but Sally wouldn't tell her husband where she was. She agreed to meet him at my office the next afternoon.

I had heard the story up to this point from Fred over the phone, and wondered what had happened to frighten Sally. Fred told me that he had never hit his wife, but there was a clear undertone of violence in his story.

They met in my waiting room, and I sneaked a look at their reunion before going out to introduce myself. Fred was a funny combination of contrite and angry as he tried to embrace his wife. She allowed him to touch her but was clearly uncomfortable. Was she frightened of him? Had he hurt her? I didn't know, but I knew right away that we had to set up some rules to protect her.

As they followed me to my office, I could feel their tension. Sally waited for Fred to sit, and then chose another couch, using the furniture to separate herself from her husband. They were an attractive couple, dressed for success. His suit looked well cut and expensive, and she wore her version of a power suit. They looked at me. I asked them to start, careful to look at both of them, so that I could tell who was elected as speaker for their crisis.

"I don't know what happened," said Fred softly. "All I know is that she left me for nothing. This is crazy." Sally looked at him as he spoke. She seemed unsure of how to respond. Fred looked directly at her. "What happened, Sal?"

He didn't sound guilty. Did that mean that he hadn't threatened her, or that he didn't think he'd done anything wrong? What had scared her?

Sally gazed at her hands, twisting them in her lap. She spoke softly. "You know my father used to hit me." He nodded. "He used to terrify me. He would stomp around and yell and then, when he'd worked himself up, he'd haul off and slap me in the face." She paused, then whispered, "You scared me."

Fred's face went white. "You thought I was going to hit you?" He sounded amazed. "I would never hit you. What were you thinking of?"

"I wasn't thinking. I just reacted. I was scared, and I bolted." Sally was embarrassed by her reaction of two nights previously, but it made perfect sense to her. She had needed to protect herself, and that's what she'd done.

"I don't believe this! I am not your father!" Fred's voice was full of anger. "Don't lump me in the same category as that man."

I could see what was happening here. Fred was going to get more and more insulted. Sally was going to withdraw when he didn't understand what was simple and obvious to her. This conversation would go nowhere. I intervened. "Sally, your father used to scare you and then hurt you." She nodded. "So when Fred scared you, you were afraid that he would hurt you, too."

"I don't know why. He's never threatened me. But I got scared. I'm sorry, Fred. It's not about you. I was just too frightened."

"Of me? Why of me? I never hurt a woman and I'm not about to start now." He sounded less angry but not yet calm. Fred was truly offended.

"Not of you. But right then I just knew I was in danger. And since then, I've been scared that I hurt your feelings. So I couldn't face you."

Now there were two issues on the table. The Parkes were not complaining of marital violence, but of her fear of being hit. They were also trying to figure out how to reconnect after a major blowup. How could Sally return to Fred? Did he deserve an apology? Did she? How could they repair the damage inflicted in this fight?

Fighting, like every part of a couple's interaction, follows rules that we learned in our original families. Sally "knew" that men hit girls when the men were angry, so she "knew" she was in danger as Fred got louder and more agitated. Fred "knew" that men don't hit women, so he "knew" that his wife was in no danger from him. But they "knew" different facts.

"Sally, when did you start to get scared?" I wanted to explore what had happened so that I could help them establish fighting rules to avoid a repeat of this situation.

"When Fred started stomping around."

"I wasn't stomping! I just moved across the room because I was upset! You really overreacted! This is crazy!" Fred sounded accusatory. I held up my hand.

"Fred, wait. You and Sally both need to know what frightened her. Neither of you wants to have another episode like this." I hoped he could keep his temper under control. Sally had the right to explore her panic without worrying about his reaction. He nodded, but I could see he was having trouble keeping himself under control. We would return to his feelings later. They both looked at me, avoiding each other's gaze.

"So what happened, Sally?"

"I was scared. I sat as still as I could, hoping he would calm down. But it didn't work. He got more and more upset. He looked so big. I felt my heart racing. Suddenly, I was on my feet and out the door. I just needed to get away."

"What were you thinking?"

"That I needed to get away. That's all." She sounded subdued and quiet. Her voice was almost a whisper.

Fred stared at his wife. "Did you really think I would hurt you?" He sounded astonished.

"I didn't think. I just reacted. Honey, I don't think now that you were going to hit me, but I *wasn't* thinking. I was just so scared!" She was confused by her own reaction. "I never would have married you if I'd felt in any danger—but I was so scared. I couldn't think, not then." I noticed that she kept repeating *scared,* a word that sounded childish coming from such a sophisticated woman. It made me wonder whether she felt childish as she recounted the quarrel. Or had she felt like a little girl during the fight?

I asked Sally to be specific. "What happened right before you panicked?"

"He started walking toward where I was sitting." Sally knew exactly what had triggered her panic. We had to start from there.

"You were OK while he was getting angry, until he walked toward you?"

"Yes." She sounded firm and sure. "When he stood up, when he came toward me, I was just too scared to manage it. I knew he was mad, but I could listen to him until he came at me."

"I didn't come *at* you. I just walked over to you. You're acting as if I'm an abuser, as if I hit women, like your crazy dad!"

"But you can't come at me! I was too scared! You need to stay away when you're mad."

The conversation was stuck. The Parkes weren't listening to each other. Sally kept telling Fred that he had scared her; Fred kept saying that he wasn't scary. He was insulted and needed to change her perception of her danger during the fight so that she would acknowledge that he was predictable, safe. Sally needed Fred to understand that she had been frightened, regardless of her trust in him. They needed to recognize that they could have widely different opinions about the fight and still listen to each other.

"Wait," I said. "What if both of you are right?" The Parkes wheeled around to look at me. "I mean it. What if you're both making sense? What if Sally was scared and Fred wasn't scary?"

"How could that be?" Fred's voice sounded contemptuous. He glanced at his watch, as though he wanted to stop wasting his time with such a crazy therapist! Sally looked unsure but hopeful. She wanted a resolution of the debate, but she couldn't understand what I was getting at.

"Well, maybe Sally was just scared," I continued, "not because you're like her father, but because she only knows men through the example of her father. Maybe she does trust you, but when the stakes are higher, as they are in a fight, she reverted to what she knows deep down—that men are dangerous when they're angry. She wasn't accusing you of getting ready to hit her. She was assuming that any man, under stress, was hazardous. Fred, maybe it had nothing to do with you at all!"

Sally nodded. "I think that's right," she said slowly. "I didn't think about you being my Fred. You were just too scary."

"But that's not fair," Fred protested. He was right. Sally was responding to her husband as though he were another person, a threatening man from her past. It wasn't fair, but it was reality. She might be able to stop her instinctive response, but not immediately and not easily. What could the Parkes do until that time arrived? What about their next fight, and the ones after that?

The Parkes needed to establish some ways of fighting that would allow Sally to feel safe, even when Fred got angry. Fred had to be allowed to get mad and Sally had to be able to work with him when he was incensed. Each had to respect the other's need. They had to be able to struggle with each other without Sally disappearing. Fred had to be assured that he could get angry at his wife and not worry that she would leave him. They had to find some new rules for fighting, ones they could live with, ones that would protect them from an escalation to separation.

Creating rules for fighting is one of the essential tasks of early marriage. We have to find acceptable ways to disagree, to lose our temper, to vent our anger at our mate. Each individual comes to marriage with a set of expectations of what happens when fights occur; the rules are unspoken and often unshared. Sally Parke, for example, was trained to fight under a set of rules that included permission for men to vent their rage physically. Her husband didn't share this expectation, and was surprised when she applied it within their marriage.

It is a pity, but we do not create these rules by sitting down and negotiating them in a reasonable fashion. We do not tell our partner what we expect him to do in a quarrel, nor do we share what we want. Instead, we react instinctively, exploding and withdrawing according to our training. This training most often has been carried out in the laboratory of our original families. We are usually unaware of its nuances unless and until it is strained by later relationships. So Sally did not know that she "expected" Fred to hit her—not until she was already scared.

Because the Parkes had no conscious awareness of what they unconsciously "knew," they could not anticipate their reactions and establish limits for their behavior in a quarrel. Sally could not warn Fred about her deep fears of angry men, and Fred was unable to prepare his wife for his pacing, a simple physical manifestation of his frustration. Each interpreted the other's behavior based on his and her personal histories. Even though they now knew what behavior might be expected in a future fight, they were still arguing about the meaning of their actions, rather than trying to solve the problems the actions caused.

"Wait a minute," I instructed. "Let's say that Sally is frightened, whether or not Fred is actually going to hurt her, even if she has no reason, at least in the present, to be scared. What do you do about it?" I addressed the question to both of them, recognizing that the problem was shared, regardless of where it started. In fact, our individual histories do create issues for the conduct of a couple—and the couple must share responsibility for creating the solution. Though this situation may have been ignited by Sally's past, the resolution had to come from both Sally and Fred.

They looked at each other, silently. I could tell that my question had stumped them. Each was still ready to debate the validity of Sally's fears, but I knew that would lead nowhere fast. I rephrased my last statement. "How can Sally feel safe? How can Fred express his anger?"

Sally laughed nervously. "I've been thinking about this a lot since I left. I know what I want, but it seems silly. Absurd, even."

"What do you want?" Fred asked. He looked at her directly.

"I will do what I can—I just don't want you to leave again!" Fred was setting his own rules now. He needed to be able to fight with his wife without the threat of her disappearance.

"I want you to sit down. To stay sitting down. I want you to stay still."

Fred smiled. "That's all? To stay in a chair?"

"Yes." Sally had been all right in the fight until her husband got up from his seat, at which point she felt threatened and scared. She thought about what would make her feel safe, secure. This was her solution.

We looked at Fred. Could he accept this? He smiled. "I can do that." He paused. "But I need to know that you won't leave me." He was negotiating what he needed—a reasonable exchange.

Sally looked uncomfortable. She shifted in her seat as she pondered his request. "I want to promise that. I really do. But I didn't know I was going to leave. I didn't think about it or decide to go. How can I promise to stay when I only left out of terror?"

"I won't scare you. Not again," Fred promised.

Sally was being very careful. She was unwilling to give Fred a guarantee that she might not be able to deliver. "I can try. I want to say I can promise, but I think I can only promise to try." I could see that this was difficult for Fred. He definitely wanted a guarantee. With a sigh, he nodded. Then he reached out his hand to Sally. He needed to touch her, to seal the bargain, to re-establish a working relationship through contact. She smiled and took his hand.

Rules for Fighting

The Parkes had begun the difficult task of establishing rules for fighting. What makes this so hard?

We need rules for all aspects of our relationships, but possibly none is as important as those related to fighting. For our intimate quarrels, we need to know that we are safe, both physically and psychologically. We need to know how to start a fight and how to end it, what is acceptable to say, and whether words can be forgotten or forgiven. We need to know when and where a fight can happen, and whether it may be public or must be private. We need to know the meaning of silence, how to interpret it as thoughtfulness or rejection. And we need to know whether, even in the depths of rage, we are still loved.

Establishing guidelines for intimate conflict can be done quickly, but revisions often are made slowly. We tend to follow the rules of our original families, discussing only those aspects which are unshared with our mate. It may be better, however, if we find ways to discuss what we need and want at other times— away from an emotional maelstrom.

> EXERCISE 23: Remember your last fight with your partner. Where did it take place? In the car, at home, on the phone, at a friend's house? What time of day did it begin? When did it end? Who was angrier? How did you bring the fight to a close? How did you reconnect? How long did the bad feelings last?

If we dissect the pattern of our fighting, then we can start the process of creating and refining rules for fighting. I do not believe there are many unbreakable rules, but no fair fight can take place under the threat of physical violence or emotional humiliation. I tell couples clearly and unequivocally that any violence must be followed immediately by a call to the police. Neither party in a couple engaged in a fight that turns violent is capable of defusing or altering it as quickly or effectively as the police can. In fact, I will not work with violent couples unless they sign a promise that any physical threats will instantly lead to police protection.

Sally Parke had not done this, although she did the next best thing: she got out. Sometimes creating physical space between battling adults serves the same purpose as calling the police. However, if there is a pattern of actual violence, I believe that is an inadequate response.

It is essential that couples understand that violence against objects—breaking plates or glasses, hitting the walls—is a form of physical violence. If you are in such a situation, you must get out and call the police immediately. It is not reasonable to wait to discuss what's going on. No one should ever remain in a situation where there is a threat of violence.

The other unbreakable rule concerns emotional humiliation. This is harder to measure, as each of us has a different threshold. For some of us, particular words have huge emotional weight, carrying meanings that are more hurtful than the actual definition of the word. These words must be acknowledged as off-limits in an intimate quarrel. So you may not be allowed to call your partner stupid, or tell him to shut up, or make fun of her language. Another person might not be so wounded by these phrases, but your partner's vulnerabilities must be respected, even in moments of intense emotion! The purpose of a quarrel is not—and cannot be—to triumph over your partner; it is to solve a problem.

For many couples, this is a difficult concept. Intimate arguments may seem like battles to the death. Despite the intensity of emotional tangles, however, the individual must respect the needs and hot spots of the partner. Arguments with partners are different from any other fight we engage in— because the cost of winning may be greater than the cost of losing. If either individual is damaged in an intimate quarrel, the injury may last longer and be more severe than the original cause. If one spouse is deeply hurt, the trust between the partners may be destroyed. Trust is an essential part of intimacy, and must not be crushed in the urge to "beat" each other in the heat of anger. Fighting, when carried out with care, may actually increase intimacy—but only when we take care of our mate's needs as well as our own.

Fighting as Intimacy

It is surprising to many couples that arguing can enhance intimacy. In fact, we often say the most personal things to each other under the stimulus of anger. Intense emotion often permits us to say what we really mean, even those thoughts we have been hiding from our mates. If both mates are respectful and careful, their fighting can become an essential part of their caring.

> EXERCISE 24: With whom do you fight? What is permissible to say to your parents, best friends, spouse, siblings? Have you engaged in an argument that led to a feeling of increased intimacy? How did that happen?

Most of us fight within the boundaries of our most intimate relationships, with the people we trust the most, the people who can see us when we're furious, tearful, or simply nutty. They are the people who hear our thoughts before they're completely formed, who watch us struggle with important decisions, who disagree with our opinions, and whose ideas we value most highly. Fighting is only one of the ways we mark the intimacy of a relationship—and it should not be the only one. Arguments happen in most, if not all, intimate relationships.

Although we must accept quarrels as a necessary part of our closest relationships, we need not accept all fighting behavior. Each of us has expectations and needs for certain kinds of conduct in emotionally charged situations. These needs are integral to our negotiations over the rules of argument. We have to develop guidelines for discussion, standards that increase respect for oneself and the other, standards that allow us to be critical and still be close, standards that force us to listen to each other.

Why Do We Fight?

It is important to understand that fighting does serve a purpose. While the experience of quarreling may be unpleasant, your understanding of what makes your spouse angry helps you to know that person better. In fact, when couples tell me that they never fight, I always wonder why not, since arguments are essential to intimate interaction.

We fight for many reasons. The most obvious one is that quarreling blows off steam between a couple, allowing them to dispel emotional and physical anger. In a wonderful old children's book, *The Quarreling Book,* each person is hurt by the nastiness of the preceding person, and is therefore mean to the next person—as though this makes the original hurt easier to bear!

Sometimes we fight because we need to say awful things to our mates, things so hurtful that they frighten us. All of us know at a subliminal level that words said in a loud tone of voice are poorly heard, that when we yell, our partner hears the tone but not the words. I believe that men especially are intimidated by the decibel level of their spouses. So some of our fights allow us to tell our partners those things they cannot hear—and in a manner in which they cannot hear them. For example, in the context of a loud argument, a woman may tell her husband that he is getting fat or that she hates his friends. He is unlikely to hear the content of her words, but she will feel that she has expressed her anger. Such arguments are unlikely to produce change, but they are not supposed to. Their goal is to allow one partner to say things in a way that the other partner cannot hear.

The importance of this idea escapes many couples; we feel

that we communicate extremely vital ideas in the heat of passion. The problem is that we cannot hear much of what is said at a high decibel level.

For most of us, the experience of being yelled at is simply a lot of frightening noise. Although we do not hear the words, we hear the scary sounds of our partner's anger. Being yelled at makes us feel small and vulnerable. It raises our anxiety and lowers our ability to process information.

EXERCISE 25: Remember a time when your parents yelled at you. What were they angry about? How did you feel? Frightened? Did you understand what they were trying to say, or just feel that they were scary?

Surprisingly, we fight to connect with our mates. A disagreement, whether loud or quiet, passionate or detached, gives us the opportunity to tell other people who we are and what we need. These intimate exchanges are our chance to be close and connected, to help shape the course of our relationship, to express our love and our disappointment.

Gender Differences

Men and women process anger in very different ways. While this may be a generalization, I believe that anger is often easier for women. Men tend to be overwhelmed by their anger, experiencing it at a physical level. Women are better able to vent their feelings through the use of language. Arguments may escalate through words, comfortable for women, to a level where men are frightened by their body's reactiveness. Women can cry and scream—behaviors frowned on for men—which help them release tension. Men who do not have these outlets are often overwhelmed by fights.

I frequently see men who withdraw when fighting begins.

This behavior, which often infuriates the partner and therefore intensifies the fight, is an attempt to control both the emotional level of the interaction and the man's growing physical discomfort. It usually backfires. Typically, the woman will continue to yell—and may yell louder to try to involve her withdrawn partner. The spiral continues until one party breaks the pattern, through rage, tears, or withdrawal. Both individuals leave such bouts feeling bruised and misunderstood.

Tape-Recorded Fights

The McDunns walked into my office for their fourth appointment. Kathleen was a plump housewife, her long hair pulled back in an elastic band. She was dressed, as always, in jeans and a sweater, and she took her usual spot on my long green couch, where she waited expectantly.

Pat followed his wife, waiting for me to enter the room before he came in. He was tall, with red hair, freckles, and red cheeks. His sense of humor was demonstrated by his bright red socks, mostly hidden by a gray suit.

The McDunns were a young couple with a small child. They had been high school sweethearts in their small Ohio town. Then they went to college together and married the day after graduation. Kathleen worked to put Pat through law school. When he got his first job, she stayed home, and their daughter, Jillian, was born a year later.

Pat worked long hours at his law firm. He was happy and challenged at work. Kathleen enjoyed being home with Jillian, now an energetic three-year-old. Their lives took parallel routes. There were no big surprises until Pat was offered a new job— back in Ohio.

Kathleen had seemed ambivalent about returning to the Midwest. She said she felt that the major part of the decision was Pat's—"It's his job, after all"—but she had become angry and explosive. Pat called me to get his wife into therapy. He was surprised when I asked him to come in with Kathleen, but he joined her in my office.

In the first three sessions, the McDunns had talked about their lives and their history. They told me that they were fighting a lot more than in the past, but I never had any sense of high tension or stress. It had seemed strange that they were complaining of problems while they acted the happy, contented couple. I had no way of knowing that their demeanor would change today.

Pat started, as usual; he was clearly the spokesperson. "I've had it. She's so nasty to me—and now it's even directed at Jillian. We just won't move, if that's what Kathleen wants." He sounded angry and hurt, but he seemed to be conceding his major goal up front. Why was he giving up?

Kathleen looked at me, then back at her husband. Her face was stony. I could see anger for the first time. "It would be different if you'd try to understand. But all you want is a decision!" Her words came out like bullets aimed at her husband. "Think about how I feel, why don't you?"

Pat's voice slowed, got quieter. I could tell that he was trying to control the amount of emotion in the room. "Tell me what you want. I don't know what you want to do."

"Does it matter what I want? It's your job—and that's how we live."

Pat looked hurt. "Of course it matters. You matter." His sentences were getting shorter, his voice subdued. He was withdrawing emotionally, unable to tolerate his wife's anger. "Just tell me what you want." Pat obviously wanted this quarrel to end—and end quickly. But he did not know what to do to bring about closure. He seemed increasingly uncomfortable.

I interrupted. "Tell me how the quarrel usually goes." Couples are often surprised by this request. In fact, I am asking the couple to observe themselves so that, rather than have the fight, they can describe the fight. All of us know how such fights go in our intimate relationships. We can easily predict the sequence of accusation and reconciliation.

I call this predictable pattern a "tape-recorded fight." These are the angry outbursts that follow an expected plan. The McDunns knew what each of them would say and what response to anticipate. While the tape-recorded fight allowed them to blow off steam about this difficult issue, it blocked the possibility of resolution. Kathleen would multiply her accusations of Pat's excessive power to make decisions, and Pat would argue unsuccessfully that he wanted her suggestions. But nothing would change.

Change is the goal of therapy, and it is one of the most exciting byproducts of marriage. But our tape-recorded fights deny the possibility of change. I think, indeed, that this is the primary purpose of tape-recorded fights: to keep the couple safe from too much change, too fast. What happens is simple. The McDunns, faced with a difficult decision, were unable to resolve the problem without putting the desires of one over the desires of the other. Instead of choosing Pat over Kathleen or Kathleen over Pat, they fought about a side issue: the issue of his job. This issue, although difficult, was less frightening than the real problem: where they would live.

EXERCISE 26: What issues do you use for tape-recorded fights? How do these fights progress? Who says what to whom? How do you know when the quarrel is over?

Some of the hallmarks of tape-recorded fights were obvious in Pat and Kathleen's discussion. They were flinging accusations without any expectation of being heard, and they knew what would happen next, so they didn't have to pay attention! I knew we had to interrupt the pattern. "What would happen if you tried to have this discussion differently?"

Kathleen looked at me. "What do you mean? Different how?"

"If you stayed with the problem and tried to solve it." Their faces, full of expectation a moment before, fell. Usually couples have tape-recorded fights because they anticipate that they cannot solve the problem. Patterned discussions like this often occur in an area a couple feels powerless to change. Part of my job is to help them approach the problem in a new way so that they can find a solution. "What's the *real* problem?"

"We want different things. Pat wants this new job, and I want him home more."

Pat wheeled toward Kathleen. "What do you mean?"

"Well, you said you're happy about going home so that I can be with my parents and your parents. But I want to be with you! And if we move, you'll spend more time at work and hope that they'll take care of Jillian and me. I don't want that."

"I thought you'd want to be closer to home! You always say you miss Ohio, and you always want to vacation there. Don't you want to go back?"

"I don't know. Not now that it's a possibility. What will happen to *us* if we go back there?"

Suddenly the McDunns' quarrel had changed shape. They were talking about the issue, not accusing each other. They had something to work on, something they could solve. Now they could talk to each other, solve the problem. The fight had served its dual purpose, first distracting them and then getting them to focus on the issues.

How Do Fights Happen?

Most of our quarrels follow predictable patterns. The specifics of a particular fight will vary, depending on its importance, each individual's stress and tiredness, and the rules the couple develops for resolving intimate debates. We can get stuck in every part of a fight, so we need to understand what happens when we quarrel. Remember that each of us evaluates the segments of our arguments differently, and what may be explosive to you may seem benign to your mate. The general pattern can be described as follows:

- Our fights begin with a SIMMER. This period, before any direct expression of anger or disappointment, is when we are getting angry. It feels uncomfortable, but we may not know why or what's going on. Sometimes people get nasty during this period. It may be very quick—in people with a short fuse—or long and drawn out. Either way, most of us are aware of our discomfort without understanding its cause. For the McDunns, the simmer was their growing distance from each other, exacerbated by the assumptions each made about the partner's wishes.

- The next period is the EXPLOSION. It is marked by a dramatic increase in tension, often through a confrontation. Someone feels very angry and expresses it. The partner who isn't yelling may be surprised and shocked at the explosion. Pat and Kathleen's explosion occurred at the possibility of a return to Ohio, but was not simply a reaction to that idea. The explosion could have occurred about any number of issues, especially in a situation like this, where the couple had been sending warning signals.

- The third portion of the sequence is the REACTION. The partner who has not initiated the conversation responds to the explosion of the other. This reaction will have a huge impact on the development of the argument. The reactor may yell back, defend himself, or become silent. Silence is one of the most effective—and most unfair—weapons we use in our intimate relationships. It implies, basically, "I don't need to respond to you. Your feelings aren't important enough for me to waste my time on." Small wonder that silence makes people furious!

- The fourth part of the quarrel is VENTING. For some couples, this goes on for a long period of time; for others, it is over almost as soon as it begins. This is when we say what we are thinking, often over and over. Venting can lead to more explosions and heightened anger, or it may begin the transition to the next stage. The McDunns were stuck in this stage. They were able to express themselves, but without any lessening of the tension.

- The fifth step is COOLING OFF. For many couples, there are rituals that mark the beginning of this stage. One of the partners may leave the room, begin to cry, or move closer to the other. We tell each other that it's time for the fight to end, even if there's been no resolution of the precipitating issue. It is important for each partner to learn the mate's way of saying, "I'm ready to calm down."

- The sixth step, often referred to as the best part of a fight, is RECONCILIATION. It is essential that partners find a way to reconnect after a blowup. In the case of Sally Parke, she did not know how to come home, to get back with her husband after their fight. Couples must develop rituals to bring themselves back into contact. Our popular literature tells us that sex is an effective way to re-establish the relationship. It may be, but it is only one of many. Couples may touch, talk, or engage in some other nurturing activity. It is, after all, the togetherness that helps us remember why we're in the relationship in the first place!

- The final stage is often the hardest to evaluate: EFFECT. For a fight to be meaningful, to serve a purpose, something should be accomplished. What happened because of this quarrel? In some sense, effect asks, "What did we learn?" All our fights, we hope, give us information and ideas about what we should—and should not—do in the future. For a fight to be helpful for anything other than blowing off steam, there should be at least a minimal effect.

Effective Fighting

What do we have to do to make our fighting useful rather than destructive? First, we must use all our communication skills, because arguing is a form of communication. But fighting is a distinct kind of emotional exchange and may require more attention to basic rules, which we should follow in our heated arguments. Remember, these are easier said than done!

Stay on task. If you're fighting about something that happened today, what happened three weeks ago is generally irrelevant. Most of us bring in other occasions and other slights when we feel as though we're losing. Keep to the issue at hand; move on to other topics when this one is resolved. If there is a pattern of behavior you want to talk about, lay out the entire problem in as calm a manner as possible.

Don't accuse. When we are assaulted with complaints, most of us respond by becoming defensive, unable to hear what the other person is saying. Talk about what the problem is—for you. It is much more effective to tell your partner your problem, because then your mate will try to help.

Be respectful. Name-calling and humiliation are never necessary or useful.

Listen to each other, and respond to each other. This is difficult for people who are enraged but it is essential. When your partner communicates, you must listen and respond.

Talk about yourself, not about your partner. Remember the basics of communication, and say what you *know*. We do not know what other people think and feel, but we know what we think and feel. Don't read your partner's mind. Explain yourself!

Participate. When half of a couple has a problem, the couple has a problem. Remember that you're in this marriage together. Do not detach yourself from your mate; that is destructive behavior!

Remember to respect and protect the marriage as well as your position. Winning is not the goal, for you may win the battle but lose the war. The beneficial outcome of marital fights is to become closer, more intimate, more caring. If you do damage to your partner, you disturb and may injure his or her ability to engage in a trusting relationship.

SUGGESTIONS FOR FURTHER THOUGHT

- Think of fights you've had with your parents, siblings, friends, or boss. Is there one type of behavior that sets you off, or are your fights particular to each person, relationship, or situation?

- How do these fights differ from fights with your partner? Are there different limits to your behavior in fights with your partner? Are there behaviors you practice with other people that might be helpful with your spouse?

- Sometimes disagreements occur at inappropriate times. Do you and your partner have a way to agree to postpone a fight?

> The prince and Cinderella came together in the heat of infatuation. They met, danced, fell in love, and married. Now they have to find ways to live together, to share each other's triumphs and losses, to be the support each needs. They have to love each other deeply, to become intimate friends.

9

SEX AND OTHER FORMS OF INTIMACY

IF THE 1980S WERE KNOWN AS THE ME DECADE, then the 1990s should be called the Intimacy Decade. My office is full of people who strive for intimacy, often without any clear sense of what intimacy is or how people achieve it. These individuals and couples are frustrated and unhappy that they aren't intimate, but cannot seem to repair the problem.

What is intimacy? For each of us, the actions that lead to intimacy are different, but the experience is a universal one. It is those fleeting moments when we feel truly understood and appreciated. These moments may take place in bed, during a wonderful conversation, looking at a beautiful sunset, or when nothing of consequence is otherwise happening. They are priceless moments—the high points of our lives. Sometimes they occur while we are alone, perhaps recalling past events or fantasizing about the future. Sometimes they happen at major life events, at a marriage or the birth of a child. Sometimes they are associated with the saddest times of our lives, when the touch of a loved one reminds us of our connection and of caring.

Moments of intimacy are critical to the health of a marital relationship, but they are *not* reliable. Intimacy often happens when we least expect it—after a particularly emotional movie or in the midst of a nasty fight. It is hard to plan for intimacy, to create intimate interludes. And each of us expresses our needs for intimacy differently.

> EXERCISE 27: Remember a recent moment of real intimacy. How did it begin? What was the setting? How long did it last? How did you feel, about yourself and about your partner?

Intimacy is one of the stickiest concepts we must master in marriage. It involves both closeness and separateness, warmth and distance. It occurs randomly, but what it requires is far from random. What it requires is the awareness of our partner as a completely separate human being.

Separate but Connected

To connect with another person, we must understand that he or she is different from ourselves. Just because I love my husband does not mean that I agree with him about a particular idea, or even that I think his position has merit. It does mean, however, that I am interested in his ideas, that I will listen to him with respect and caring, and that I will not make fun of him.

If attachment meant sameness, love would be the ultimate act of narcissism. Real love, in fact, acknowledges the differences between partners. Loving someone, despite differences, is deeper love than the infatuation that requires agreement. Couples often have difficulty with the concept that lovers should accept and celebrate their differences, because it is counter to our cultural expectations. But it is an essential idea—love must accept contrasts!

Our need for distinction in our emotional relationships seems innately contradictory. We hope that our intimate partners see the world as we do, sharing our perceptions of other people, of good vacation spots, of favorite dinners. In truth, our shared journey is enhanced by differences. Variety helps us grow and question, change and adapt. It keeps relationships young and vibrant. And it seems to be what fascinates all of us; hence the famous expression "Opposites attract."

We see these differences between mates in many ways, but none so clearly as in our need for intimacy. Each of us has different needs for—and tolerance of—closeness, and each of us expresses the need differently. Sometimes we let our mates know that we want closeness by snuggling and sharing. Surprisingly, I think we are just as likely to ask for intimacy by berating our spouses, complaining about the distance between us. This is rarely effective. No one wants to get close to an angry, complaining mate, even if that person is trying to request intimacy.

Staying Close; Staying Distant

David Marques had been in individual therapy with me for almost a year—a long time for a client of mine. He had worked hard to understand his family of origin and their influence on his present-day life. His parents had divorced when he was a small child, and he was raised by his mother's sister, Aunt Terry, and her widowed mother. David adored both women; he believed that they had saved him from the wrath of his erratic mother and his neglectful father. He felt they were all that stood between him and abandonment. He was probably right.

But Aunt Terry and Grandma also sounded like Tartars. They taught David all about how to eat with the correct fork and how to behave himself in public, but they never tucked him in at night. They never held him when he cried that his mother and father didn't send him birthday presents. They didn't go to Parents' Day at school, because they weren't his parents. He went off to college at eighteen with a mixed sense of relief and loneliness.

This loneliness followed him for the next ten years. He saw Aunt Terry and Grandma at holiday times, but he never felt any sense of connection to them or to anyone else. And then Grandma died. David was sad, but not very sad. This worried him, and he found himself evaluating his life. He was successful, but he was still lonely. He had friends he could go drinking with, but no one he felt comfortable talking to. His life felt sterile. He had never had a serious relationship with a woman. He was approaching thirty without a clear sense of what he wanted or how to get it. So he started therapy.

After almost a year, David understood a lot more about himself. He realized that he could be grateful to his two rescuers, even though he also felt deprived by them. He knew that people scared him, and that he could strive to overcome this fear. Having been raised by two female relatives, he began to understand that he was not sure what being male really meant to him. And he knew he would have to work at being with other people, to overcome his basic distrust. He even talked to Aunt Terry about how sad he had been as a child. She listened to him and made him feel cared for. He was almost content.

David and I both knew that he was waiting for a relationship with a woman. He needed someone to love him and a place to feel valued. So we were both happy when he bounced into my office one day and proclaimed that he had met "the greatest lady."

"She's wonderful! She's smart and pretty and she can talk to me really easily. She can even get me to talk to her! It's as if we've known each other all our lives. Her name is Daisy and she could be my best friend right now!"

I had a powerful urge to slow him down, to try to dampen his enthusiasm. It seemed to me almost dangerous—as though he were careening down a road at high speed. But I felt sure that I would have little impact on his excitement, so I merely asked, "Tell me about her."

"She's twenty-five and she's a singer. She's trying to make a name for herself, but it's hard for someone so young. I met her last week at a singles party, and she has lots of friends and, guess what? She lives at home—so I know she has a good relationship with her mother." I could tell that this really appealed to David: a woman who was in a family. Just what he had been searching for!

Daisy's mother, Tess, liked David a lot. She was very supportive of the relationship between him and Daisy. He ate dinner at their house a few times a week, and she sometimes joined them when they went to the movies. He was always included in family celebrations. David understood that there was some tension between Daisy and her mother, but he attributed this to the typical mother-daughter relationship. He remembered the occasional blowups between Grandma and Aunt Terry, and decided that all mothers and daughters fought. He liked both women, and he especially liked being in their family.

David and Daisy dated seriously for some months. She sounded like a great match for him. He described her as a woman with high expectations, and he felt he could learn a great deal from her. Soon they were talking about living together, and then the troubles began.

Tess seemed very happy when David and Daisy began looking for an apartment to share. She advised them about how to read the want ads, and even asked to go along on drive-bys, to see neighborhoods and apartments. David was surprised that Daisy objected to her mother's company, but allowed her to override his desire that Tess accompany them. Daisy and David looked and looked and looked. They had a lot of trouble agreeing on the "perfect" place to live.

After a month of looking, Tess suggested that David move in with her and Daisy on a temporary basis. David was unsure. He came in to a regular session and asked me what I thought. I turned the question back to him.

"What's the issue?" I asked.

"I don't know. I just feel funny about it."

"Because you'll be having sex in her mother's house?"

"I don't know. I don't think it's that. I just think it's strange."

"What does Daisy think?"

"That's just it. She keeps saying it's up to me. I can't figure out what's going on with her and Tess." He looked worried. He ran his hand through his curly hair and sighed. "I want to do the right thing, but I don't know what that is. I mean, what would it be like, living with Tess? And why doesn't Daisy have an opinion?"

In my mind, the last question was the really important one. Daisy, not David, knew what it was like to live with Tess. Why was she avoiding this important decision? David was clearly picking up her ambivalence, and it was making him more confused. How could he decide such an important issue on his own? And why should he have to? This seemed a really bad move.

"What does Daisy say? Why does she want you to decide?" I asked.

"It's weird. She says it matters more to me than it does to her. Because of growing up the way I did." He paused, his face reflecting his struggle to put his feelings into words. "She says I need a family. And I know that I do. But does she want to live with Tess? Why is she being so unclear?"

That was a very good question. Daisy was being evasive, and she was being so for a reason. David couldn't understand what that was. Daisy obviously needed David to make the decision for her. Was she afraid to move out of her mother's home? Did she need her mother's support to live with David? How could David and Daisy resolve this question? They not only needed to come to a conclusion that would work for them, but also needed to create a way to solve a difficult problem, one that might very well shape their future negotiations. I thought that David's confusion was completely understandable.

The next day, David called and asked whether Daisy could join us for a session. They came in two days later. I was curious to meet Daisy, wondering how I would view her. She was exactly as he had described her. Her hair was long and curly, framing a small face with huge gray eyes. She was physically petite, but she felt larger than she was; her presence was powerful. I assumed her presence worked to her advantage as a singer. She was hard to look away from.

David started. "I don't know why this has gotten so important. I don't want to make the wrong decision, but I don't know what the right decision is. Daisy, what do you want to do?"

She seemed taken aback by his question, almost as if she had been attacked. The issue had become so large, and I was still unsure why. Daisy responded slowly. "This matters a lot to you, Dave. You look on my mother as your new family. I don't think you know what you're getting into here, but I can't stand in the way of what matters to the two of you." She looked sad, and I asked her why. "Because I know how important this family thing is to David. And Mom represents all he's ever wanted. But I don't know whether it's all I've ever wanted." David started to interrupt, and I held up my hand to stop him. Daisy continued, "Sometimes I feel left out."

This seemed to me especially sad. "Left out?" I asked.

"Yeah. Mom always wanted someone who needed her, the way David does. And that's just not me. Sometimes I feel like a fifth wheel."

David looked shocked. "No, you're the center of it all. The most important. How could you feel like a fifth wheel?" Clearly, David and Daisy had very different perceptions of their relations with Tess and of the relations between the three of them.

"Daisy, describe your mother to me. I've heard about her from David, but I want to know how you see her."

She looked at her lover, as if assessing what to say; she was being very careful. Then she began to talk, measuring her words. "My mom was widowed when I was five. My dad was a gambler, and he had no life insurance. So Mom had to work to support me. She took a secretarial job, and she hated it. She doesn't like to be told what to do, but she had to work to feed me. She worked for a big-shot lawyer, and he made her work long hours. She really sacrificed for me." I was struck by her description. She had told me very little about who her mother really was, but I noticed that she took responsibility for her mother's unhappiness. Obviously, Tess had had to work to support herself as well as her daughter, but Daisy felt culpable for her mother's hardships. She continued, confirming my suspicions. "She lived for me. She needs me to be happy so that she can feel happy. She loves me a lot."

"Too much?"

"I don't know. Can you love someone too much?"

"I guess so, don't you think?" I was trying to give her the opportunity to evaluate the question for herself, but she changed the subject.

"Anyhow, what should we do? I think David has to decide, because he's the one who needs a family. I already have one." She laughed uncomfortably and looked at David, obviously wondering why he was waiting. Then she looked at me, silently asking for help. She nervously twirled her hair around her index finger. "What? Did I miss something?"

David began to speak slowly. "Does she love you too much?" This was a new idea for him. All his life, David had wanted to be loved, to be the center of someone's world. Daisy was suddenly making him question the value of such caring. He needed to know whether she was overwhelmed by Tess.

"Sometimes I can't breathe." We all knew that Daisy was describing her relationship with her mother. "Sometimes she needs me to be happy so much, to justify what she did for me."

"That's a lot of responsibility," I said encouragingly.

She sighed, as though she were exhausted. "It's an endless responsibility."

The Two Parts of Intimacy

David and Daisy represent the two disparate parts of intimacy. In some sense, their relationship was working because each knew exactly what the other wanted. David offered Daisy the space and separation she needed but could not have within her relationship with Tess. Daisy offered David closeness. This was not yet a problem, but I could anticipate that the young couple would struggle with issues of intimacy throughout their relationship. It was time for them to learn new ideas about intimacy.

Intimacy is a composite of separateness and closeness, essentially a combination of two contradictory components. In fact, to be truly close to another person, we must acknowledge our basic differences. For many couples, this concept is difficult. Instead, we often describe our loved one by saying that the other person is just like us. "I can't tell where he stops and I begin." "We can complete each other's thoughts." "I feel as if I'm with another me." These descriptions of love are familiar to all of us. We condense love into a simple assumption of sameness.

In reality, we usually love people who are very different from ourselves. Slobs are attracted to neatniks; people who are on time seem to meet and match with those who are chronically late. My husband, who appears very organized, fell in love with a person who hates to put her clothes away and who leaves piles all over the house. When people are courting, they tend to notice similarities. We pay attention to the resemblances, because they make us feel closer, more like one person. We experience ourselves as two parts of a whole.

As relationships progress, however, we begin to see our differences more clearly—and in less flattering terms! We notice that our mate is chronically late, poorly dressed, or sloppy. Commonly, we begin to resent the very differences that we had ignored in the first place. Our cultural expectation predicts that mates share basic traits, such as cleanliness and the need for togetherness. In my experience, we tend to be attracted to others with the same value system, including political beliefs, attitudes toward money and God, and level of activism—but not necessarily those who are as early (or late) as we are. Such behavioral traits are simply less important than the basic values of our loved ones.

This makes perfect sense to me. It is certainly critical, as we pick our life's partner, that the other person view the world—in its important aspects—as we do. A right-wing radical could not have much of a relationship with a bleeding-heart liberal; their basic language and understanding of the world are too different. Religious fundamentalists and agnostics have incompatible world views. We tend to pick mates whose values overlap our own. But this does not mean that our behavior matches!

If intimacy is not sameness, then what is it? Intimacy is the result of hearing and being heard, of accepting and being accepted, by another person who knows you. It happens when you have the opportunity to say what you mean and explain misunderstandings. It is being loved for what you are, not for what the other person wishes you were. It is the ability to argue and disagree, sometimes at a high emotional pitch, without weakening the underpinnings of the relationship.

The Disappointment of Intimacy

More difficult than understanding what intimacy is, however, is accepting what it is not. It is not complete acceptance of the other person. It is not an omniscience about what the other wants or needs. It is not communication without words. It is not nirvana, the feeling that all is right in the world, that we are finally safe. Indeed, intimacy may feel dangerous. As we increasingly value the opinions of our loved ones, our risk of being hurt grows dramatically.

> EXERCISE 28: Remember the last time your partner inadvertently hurt your feelings. Did he or she do something that you would have overlooked in another person? We often judge those closest to us by a higher standard than we use for the rest of the world—because we assume that they should know better, and because it matters more to us that they understand us.

Each of us has different expectations of our partner and our intimate relationships. In fact, each of us defines intimacy differently, both in marriage and in all other relationships. It may feel intimate to share information with a certain friend, information that seems casual and unimportant when shared with someone else. Our perception of intimacy is based on the situation, the information, and the other person. And each of us can tolerate a different amount of intimacy.

> EXERCISE 29: Think about an intimate moment you shared with a close friend. You may have told your friend something important, or listened to a story about the

friend's life, or simply experienced a personal moment together. How would this experience have been different with another, less close friend? How would it have been different with your parents, your siblings, your partner?

Creating Intimacy

How do people achieve intimacy? The process is slow; it develops and changes over the course of a relationship. We never stop refining and creating intimacy. The road can be difficult to start, but it is truly rewarding to travel.

The development of guidelines for acceptable intimacy follows the same pattern as other relationship rules. Each partner begins with individual history and expectations, which are modified by interactions. Then the partners negotiate their rules, often without ever discussing what each wants and expects. For some couples, the negotiations produce permanent and unalterable rules and guidelines. For luckier pairs, the negotiations end with temporary resolutions, open to replacement when they no longer work.

David and Daisy were beginning to create an intimate relationship. They had achieved some important understanding of each other and their different needs, but they had not found a way to establish rules for talking about these differences. Intimacy requires communication and patience, the ability to say what we mean now and to change it later. The urge to be open and clear with another person is an essential component of emotional closeness.

Interestingly, sometimes the need for intimacy may make us silent. David and Daisy were trying to protect each other from difficult feelings. In the best sense, each was investing in the relationship by not rocking the boat. But this is a strategy that rarely works over the long haul. Avoidance may help us escape confusion or anger in the present, but it usually creates its own problems. Avoidance often leads to more avoidance. When we decide to make a subject off limits, we imply that the relationship cannot handle the topic. In some sense, we begin to undermine the relationship. David and Daisy were trying to protect each other, but they were also learning to feel that some ideas cannot be discussed. Their strategy of protection was more dangerous than the topic they were avoiding.

I do not mean to suggest that every issue that arises in a relationship should or must be discussed and dissected. Far from it. Every couple has to create the rules for intimacy and closeness, to provide guidelines that work for both partners.

Flexibility

Flexibility is an essential predictor of any couple's ability to create closeness. The guidelines that a couple creates for their relationship should be flexible, open to negotiation and change. It seems obvious that, as individuals grow and mature, their rules will also evolve. The nature of intimacy changes in parallel with the growth of the people in the relationship. An older couple will likely talk about topics that a younger couple does not; different things matter to them.

One of the difficult illusions about intimacy is our cultural expectation that it should just occur, that couples who are good for each other somehow know what each is thinking. This is impossible. Each of us is unique, with our own thoughts, perceptions, and ideas. Couples must learn that the need to communicate is not a failure! Intimacy is the open exchange of personal information with a loved, trusted confidant. It is feeling exposed and feeling safe at the same time. It is the ability to create and re-create understanding, the freedom to change within a relationship, the need to share. No surprise, then, that we elevate sex to the highest form of intimacy.

Is Sexuality Intimate?

Sexuality and intimacy are, for many couples, one and the same. We express our yearnings and our love through the highly charged communication of sexual behavior. We tell our partners that we admire them, that we need them, that we are committed to them.

Sexuality is a form of communication. Whether the exchange is a small kiss, a bear hug, or a passionate sexual interlude, each of us tells our lover a great deal in every physical interaction. Naked or clothed, public or private, a hand held or an arm around the shoulder, these are communications of great importance to us. But what do they mean?

Sam and Deb Franklin had been in therapy for a few weeks before they began to address issues of their sex life. They had come to see me to sort out the problems that arise for many couples before marriage—how to negotiate with in-laws, when to set limits with each other, what each expected and wanted at the wedding. We handled problems as they arose, and they were married. After the honeymoon, they returned for what I expected would be a final, wrap-up session. I was wrong.

They walked into my office and greeted each other. Deb had come from her job as an emergency room doctor, in hospital scrubs, with her frizzy hair pulled back. She looked exhausted. Her eyes were weighted down by dark circles, which stood out in the pallor of her face. I wondered when she had last slept.

Sam was a huge contrast to his new wife. Freshly showered and shaved, he wore a dark suit and a pressed white shirt. He was impeccably attired, off to a day in the circus of investment banking. There was a huge smile on his face, and I could see the relish with which he began his day. He had told me before how much he loved his work, and I could see it written all over his face. This was a true yuppie couple—accomplished, successful professionals, caught up in exciting careers.

I began the session by congratulating them on their marriage. "Was it fun?"

They looked at each other, assessing what response to give. The exchange was not a happy one; I wondered what had happened. I waited.

Sam began. "I can't explain what happened. Deb seems to be having second thoughts. Maybe she always did. But she didn't want to be with me on the honeymoon."

"I just wanted some space. You wanted to be with me all the time—and you wouldn't keep your hands off me. I had to have some control. Someone did!"

"What do you mean? I just wanted to love you!"

Something had gone terribly wrong for the Franklins. It sounded as though they had not been able to cope with the enforced closeness of a honeymoon. Sam became the one who demanded physical affection, while Deb demanded separate space. How they handled their hurt feelings now would set the tone for issues of closeness and separation in the future. We needed to understand their disrupted honeymoon.

"Tell me," I began, "were the problems mostly about time together or about sexual time together?"

They looked at each other. Couples often do this, trying to figure out who will respond to a particular question. For the Franklins, this role passed back and forth, always a good sign about a couple's freedom in communication. It indicates that the person who needs to talk will have the right to do so, rather than a rigid arrangement in which one person speaks for both parties. I knew there was important information in who spoke first.

Deb began slowly, looking at her new husband's face for confirmation of her thoughts. "I think it started with time, but it became sexual time." Sam nodded in agreement, and she picked up speed. "I'm used to being alone, a lot. I felt overwhelmed by Sam. He wanted to spend every moment with me. At night; in the shower. It was overwhelming." I noted her repetitive use of the word *overwhelming*. She needed Sam to know how much he had intruded, how hard it was for her. "I had to get some space. I just stopped sleeping with him. Having sex. So I could get away from him."

"Did that work?" I asked.

She thought for a few moments. "I guess so. I mean, it made him angry, but he backed off. Maybe too far off."

Sam nodded. "Except I wasn't angry. I was hurt. I'm still hurt." His voice got quieter and lost its expressiveness, as though he was protecting himself from his feelings. "Why didn't you just tell me how you felt?"

"I was scared. I knew it would hurt you."

"Big deal. You hurt me anyway!" Sam's hurt was turning to anger, an easier emotion to deal with. If he got mad, he could attack Deb. If he was sad or hurt, he would feel much less powerful; anger was simpler for him. Deb recoiled from his loud voice and hostile words. I wondered whether she would counterattack or back off. She chose the latter, looking down at her hands. They were capable hands, the hands of a competent doctor, one who made rapid life-and-death decisions. But those strong hands were not giving her any support in her present situation. Her eyes filled with tears.

Sam continued, "What did you think I would feel? You rejected me—and on our honeymoon!" This was deteriorating fast.

I interrupted him. "Wait a minute, Sam. Let me understand what happened. Sam, you wanted to spend the week with Deb." He nodded and tried to talk. I held up my hand, asking him to wait and let me finish. "And Deb, you wanted to be with Sam, too." She mutely agreed. "But you had different expectations of what being together meant—in terms of time apart. Sam, you wanted there to be no time spent separately. And Deb, you needed some downtime." They looked at each other, assessing the other's take on my explanation, then nodded at me. I continued. "I don't think that difference was the problem—it was only a variance in what each of you wanted. As I see it, the problem is that you only communicated the problem indirectly—through your sexual behavior. You chose not to talk to each other. So you hurt each other more, because you didn't feel the problem was one you could talk about and solve."

I waited, but it was clear that they didn't understand, so I continued. "The problem with communicating through your sexual behavior is simple. Deb, you didn't let Sam know the real problem you had—your need for downtime. Sam, you didn't know this was what Deb was telling you, so you couldn't respond to the actual problem. And you both got hurt and angry."

He looked at me, silently agreeing. "But why did we do it this way? What's wrong with us?"

This is a nearly universal reaction. Most of us think that difficulties in our sexual relationships are horrible predictors of major problems in the relationship itself. In reality, sexual difficulties are often problems in communication—where other ideas are indirectly communicated through sexuality. We all do this in positive ways—we make love to communicate love, but danger arises when we are unclear about the meaning of the communication.

EXERCISE 30: What messages do you communicate through sexuality? Your list may include lust, love, power, dependence, anger, nurturance, loneliness. As we understand what we are saying through our sexual behavior, we can begin to talk about these messages in words, too.

The other aspect of sexual communication that often suffers is our ability to tell each other what we enjoy—and don't enjoy—in our sexual behavior. Sex is very important in our culture, but many of us are without a language in which to discuss it comfortably.

EXERCISE 31: Think about what you especially enjoy in your sexual relationship. What acts are most pleasurable for you? What do you like to do? What do you like to have your partner do? How do you communicate these preferences to each other? Are your communications about sexuality primarily verbal or nonverbal? What way works best for you? What works best for your partner? Are you comfortable talking about your sexual feelings and desires?

Most of us know which sexual behaviors give us pleasure, but we find it difficult to share the information with an intimate partner. Whether we are embarrassed or ashamed, we need to learn to explain our sexual needs and wants. For, in fact, it is only when we tell each other what we want that we are likely to get it!

The Role of Sex in Marriage

Sexual behavior is only one category of intimate behavior—and for some of us it isn't particularly intimate. But it is an important, if not essential, part of the marital relationship. Our expectations of sexual behavior have changed with cultural developments. We no longer expect that sexuality is exclusively geared to the creation of a cheap labor force, or that men enjoy sex more than women. We understand that sexuality waxes and wanes over the course of marriage, often decreasing with the birth of children and increasing during vacations. We know that sexuality may take time, and that foreplay is part of the sexual experience.

Sexuality is also a part of our complicated communication process—and requires that we understand each other's nonverbal signals. Remember that I take a bath when I want to be alone. What if my husband thought that my going to take a bath was an indirect sexual overture? What if he believed I wanted him to join me in the tub? If he came into the bathroom and was romantic, I would feel intruded upon, feel that my "explicitly" requested privacy was unimportant to him. I would probably be angry and resentful—not the best lead-in for romance! He would be confused by my reaction—didn't I tell him I wanted to be sexual? We would be ripe for hurt feelings, angry words. Neither of us would achieve what we reasonably expected.

Sexual Signals

Many couples have a pattern of sexual signals that are both verbal and nonverbal. Few of us turn to our partner and say, "I want to have intercourse with you now." Instead, we use a series of gestures or actions to let our partner know of our interest. We may snuggle in a particular way, put on a sexy negligee, or use some personal slang to alert the other person to our wishes. We may drink more than usual, put an X-rated movie on the VCR, or lay silk sheets on the bed. Some people shower or shave as a sexual overture. Each couple has its own routines. We also have ways to tell our partner yes or no. Do you roll toward your partner, caress him in a certain way, put your leg over her? Do you roll away or complain about the other person's breath or beard? These are all indications of our interest in sex, and of our willingness to follow the other person's lead.

At times the sexual signals may be clear but still less than effective. One husband in my practice would always shave as a precursor to initiating sex. This made his wife furious. I was surprised at her anger over what seemed like thoughtful behavior. She felt, however, that his shaving showed a lack of consideration—that he shaved before assessing her interest. Her perception was that his shaving made their lovemaking a unilateral decision. A simple change in this pattern led to a remarkable reduction in tension. He would ask, "Should I shave?" Suddenly she felt attended to and even began to ask him to shave.

For this couple, shaving became an effective metaphor for sex. We often speak in metaphors or phrase requests as questions (Do you want to do the dishes?) or statements (The dishes need to be washed). Small wonder that our communication sometimes fails.

> EXERCISE 32: How do you know when your partner wants to make love? How do you respond when the answer is yes? When the answer is no? Is your communication verbal, nonverbal, or a combination of the two? How do you initiate lovemaking? How does your partner indicate a positive or negative response?

Many couples wonder whether their pattern of sexual behavior and frequency is normal. While different couples—and different individuals—may have disparate needs for sexual contact, our knowledge of sexual behavior in general may be of little help in our specific relationship. It is more important how two particular people feel about their lovemaking. Individuals and couples have specific sexual yearnings; we must attend to our own pleasures and desires. To do so requires that we communicate our wants, that we develop a language of sexual discussion, that we listen to our mates' messages. The rules that apply to all other intimate interactions apply in our lovemaking as well. We must find ways to exchange information, to listen to each other, and to respond to what we've heard. Sexuality may be a form of intimacy, but real intimacy involves the ability to be personal and close while respecting each other's different-ness—and doing so in a variety of ways.

SUGGESTIONS FOR FURTHER THOUGHT

- How do you define intimacy? How does your partner define intimacy? Compare and discuss your definitions—and expect them to be different!

- When have you felt closest to your partner? What can you do to foster that feeling in the future?

- Intimacy isn't always physical or verbal. Can you think of a look your partner gave you that made you feel close and connected?

- When has sex been more than sex? How have you used sexuality to communicate other feelings? Was this effective?

- Try new ways of talking about sex: in innuendo, in street slang, in writing. Does using another "language" enable you to communicate certain ideas more easily?

> How do Cinderella and Prince Charming finally
> adapt to marriage? How do they make peace with what
> marriage is——and what it isn't? How do they modify
> their perceptions of "happily ever after," so that
> they can live in contentment?

10

FINDING CONTENTMENT

WE ARE ALL FAMILIAR WITH THE EXPRESSION "marriage takes work." We use it so often that it has become part of our cultural lexicon. We hear it from talk-show hosts, clergy and therapists, our friends. But I wonder whether the expression has become so common that we no longer know what it means.

Work? Dusting is work. Work is tax law, as is changing diapers. Work is waiting tables, and writing, and changing the car's oil. If these are work, then how is marriage work?

Work? Why do we work? Most of us work to bring home a paycheck, to pay for our homes and cars, our food and vacations. It may be interesting, or even fun, but few of us want to work every day. What do we get from marriage that would make it worth the work? And how much work will it take, anyway?

In fact, the emphasis on the work of marriage seems to overlook its worth. Marriage is a balance between give and take, sacrifice and reward. The balance exists in all our intimate relationships, though in none as clearly as in marriage. To find contentment in our intimate bonds, we must begin to understand what marriage is—and what it is not.

What Is Marriage?

At its most basic, marriage is a legal contract between consenting adults. It is an agreement to provide certain things for each other—companionship, money, and sex, to name only a few. This elementary understanding of the marital contract is woefully inadequate. As we have seen throughout the book, each of us brings a personal, unspoken awareness of marriage to this otherwise objective covenant. We expect our marriage to give us joy, happiness, companionship—but each of us defines these terms differently.

On a more complex level, marriage is an emotional contract, an agreement to be available and supportive, within reason. It is an exchange of emotional goods, a promise to be concerned and involved. It is the fantasy that we can meet each other's needs, and the pledge that we will at least try to do so. It is the assurance that we will act in good faith, and interpret each other's behavior with a benign eye.

Marriage is also a journey, an adventure. It is a journey of self-discovery, of discovery of the loved one. It provides our best opportunity to understand the meaning of compromise, to learn and apply the skills of negotiation, to experience the joys and frustrations of love. It is not the solution to all problems, the panacea of all our difficulties. It is the chance to fail and the yearning to succeed. It is risk and reward, all tied up in one.

I have always been amused by Western marriage ceremonies. We promise to love and cherish each other, under any circumstances, and then we are pronounced husband and wife. Yet we are married in name only. We know very little about the rights and responsibilities of marriage. We are not husband and wife; we are explorers at the beginning of a shared journey!

Few of us can really understand the promises we make at the start of our marriage. Few of us can imagine what "for better or for worse, in sickness and in health" might mean if our spouse is stricken with a severe mental or physical disability. The oaths are, at best, theoretical promises. "I hope I will be able to love and to cherish, in sickness and in health . . ." is what we really mean.

What Can We Promise?

What are reasonable promises to make about marriage? Sadly, what we can pledge seems inadequate. We can promise to try—to try to be supportive, to try to listen, to try to understand. We can swear that we will do more than is comfortable, that we will extend ourselves. We can promise to forgive, learn together, try to adapt to each other's needs and wants. We can promise to take the long view, see the marriage as a journey to which we are committed, look beyond specific problems to the larger picture of marital negotiation and resolution.

Many couples have difficulty with the idea that we cannot promise each other eternal loyalty and commitment. We hope—no, we expect—that our intimate relationships are a guarantee that we have a psychological home base, a place where we will always be safe and loved. The truth is that this cannot be true. People in relationships change, and change is always risky.

Although we understand that people change over time, we somehow believe that our relationship will be static, predictable. I am surprised by this assessment of marriage, because I think the process of change is what makes marriage exciting. Marriage is a continuing journey of discovery—discovery of the self and of the other—a journey replete with pitfalls and triumphs. It is an adventure.

Jody and Brian Castiglione came into my office slowly. Jody, a tall, overweight woman, wore a large cross around her neck. She was physically imposing. When she began to speak, her loud voice matched her physical presence. She started with a complaint.

"Brian is boring. He has nothing to say." Her husband shifted in his seat, but she shushed him with a gesture. "I mean, being with him is just like being alone!" She looked at me, clearly expecting me to do something about this problem. "Are all husbands like this? My friends say I can't expect anything more from him, but I want more!"

"What do you want?" I noticed that my voice had become quieter. I was trying to diminish her assault on her husband.

"What I want is reasonable!" She had grown more shrill. "I want to have fun, to be interested in this man I live with!"

Jody's accusations were vague, but Brian was stricken by her words, which he seemed to have heard before. I turned to him. "Tell me your side, Brian."

He shifted on the couch and grabbed one of the loose pillows. His T-shirt was twisted by his moving about, but he didn't seem to notice. He looked down at his big workman's hands. "I don't know," he mumbled.

"See! That's all I ever hear! He doesn't know," his wife muttered, anger punctuating her words. "Wouldn't you be bored?" Jody was trying to co-opt me against Brian. I had to defuse that process and figure out how to get him to participate.

"Brian," I began, "what's going on here?" I moved toward him, encouraging him to speak. "How long have you been fighting?" I knew I had to make my questions more concrete so that he could answer me—and he needed to share in the action in my office.

"Forever. She never listens. And I'm always wrong." His voice was as dispirited as his words. "I can't do anything right. If she wants out, then let's just get it over with."

"God, you never ever listen to me! That's what you always say. Can't you understand that I don't want out? I just want you to be like Jane."

"Who's Jane?" I asked.

"Jane, Jane, Jane. She's the Second Coming of Christ!" Suddenly there was passion in Brian's voice. "She's the gold standard!"

Jody shot a nasty look at Brian, and he subsided. "Jane's my best friend. We've been friends since we were six. She always understands me—and she always has. Is that too much to expect from my husband?" She said this with contempt, as though *husband* was a dirty word. The question was rhetorical, so she was surprised when I answered her.

"Yes, I guess it is. Too much, I mean." Now she was glaring at me instead of Brian. "He can't always understand you, but he can understand you more of the time. You just have to figure out ways to tell each other what matters."

What's Too Much?

Marriage is not a solution to all that ails us. And it does take effort to make it function effectively. Jody and Brian were in a tape-recorded fight, but I was struck that they were fighting *for each other*. Jody wanted more of Brian, even though her approach of lambasting him was clearly driving him away. He was afraid to speak for fear that her anger would worsen. Brian was also in pain; he wanted to make the situation better, but he was unable or unwilling to compete with Jane. They needed to come to a mutual understanding of what they reasonably could expect from each other, now and in the future.

What we think we should get from our mates is an ideal, not a reasonable expectation at any time. We think we should be able to count on trust, thoughtfulness, honesty, reliability, constant love, and openness, to name only a few traits. These wonderful traits, however, will come and go over the course of marriage. We are all more or less trustworthy, more or less honest. We are also distractible, angry, human. A couple must establish early in marriage which traits have more room for flexibility—and which do not.

The Castigliones had established a pattern of interacting that was not working for either of them. Each was lonely for the other, unable to get what he and she had expected from marriage. Jody was gradually replacing Brian with Jane, who could easily step into his shoes. Brian was withdrawing more and more, hiding behind mumbling responses. They were stuck between what they wanted and how they had tried—and failed.

What both Jody and Brian did right was to nurture hope. They came for help because they knew something was wrong and wanted to fix it. They did not quit on their marriage.

What does marriage require? Hope. A sense of the future. Patience.

Hope

All marriages are contracts based on hope. Hope that your partner will move toward you. Hope that the two of you will be able to talk about problems, rather than act them out. Hope that you will be able to create solutions and negotiate new solutions when old ones fail. Most of us are aware of some of our hopes—the hope that our spouse will change in certain ways, the hope that we will be successful, the hope that we will maintain a close relationship with our families. But we have other, unspoken hopes, hopes that will influence our perception of our marriage. And we must have faith that we will be able to survive the rough marital terrain.

EXERCISE 33: How long do you expect to be married? How long do you hope to be married? How do you show your partner that you expect and hope to stay married? How do you know what your partner thinks about your marriage? What kind of reassurance do you offer each other? What rituals do you have that keep you on the same wavelength?

My husband and I have developed an interesting ritual. Every year, on our anniversary, we go out for a special dinner. The evening is not a simple dinner and a movie, and it is never shared with friends. It is a long meal, and we talk about lots of things—work, the kids, money. At some point, we seem to slip into a discussion that we call "The State of the Union." We talk about our marriage, about how we're doing, about what needs to change, about how each of us is feeling about the other and our relationship. While we may have a similar conversation at any point during the year, the anniversary ritual has become important to both of us. It is a space in time when we know that we will have an assessment of the other's feelings and hopes, a spoken commitment to our marriage. In some sense, it is a yearly renewal of our vows. But it is also a more realistic exchange of promises—with the increased understanding of who each of us is and is not.

The Castigliones were still trying to negotiate their relationship according to an old rule—the rule that this relationship was supposed to meet all their needs. Jody was disappointed that Brian could not fill Jane's place in her life; that he was not her only best friend. But he wasn't able to be Jane for her—nor did she really need him to fill this role. Jody had Jane. She needed

Brian to be her husband, not her best girlfriend. They had to figure out what *husband* and *wife* meant so that they could begin to fill the roles for each other.

An essential part of the exploration must be hope. Both members of the couple have to expect to be happy in the marriage, to expect the other person to do everything possible to be there. Hope does not imply that I will do everything for my husband, only that my intentions are good, that my commitment is firm, that my love will withstand the difficult tests of time. Hope is a pledge, not a guarantee.

A Sense of the Future

The Castigliones had come to marriage counseling for a simple reason: their sense that they would be together forever had been eroded by their problems in communication. They needed to re-establish their relationship so that they could regain their belief in a long-term future.

This belief in the future is essential for all relationships, whether between parent and child, friends, or mates. Without this commitment, most of us would not choose to endure the difficult times that are part and parcel of human connection. Few parents would tolerate the antics of an adolescent child unless they were aware that adolescence is only part of the road, that adulthood will bring further changes in the relationship. In fact, enduring the bad times may make the light at the end of the tunnel seem brighter, more valuable.

> EXERCISE 34: What difficult times have you and your partner survived? How did you keep connected during these stressful periods? How did you let each other know you expected to get through the hard times? How were you able to keep attached? All of us seem

inclined to focus on what we do wrong, what doesn't work. But one of the best habits in any relationship is to attend more to what does work. Understanding how you have survived a difficult or stressful time will give you lots of information about how to do so in the future.

All relationships need a sense of the future, a belief that together the couple can endure what life dishes out. But the commitment is never license for verbal or physical abuse. We must all know the limits of the bond of matrimony. There is no room to tolerate abusive behavior—and we must know that each of us defines abuse differently. What constitutes abuse to you or your mate is abuse in your relationship. We need to understand, however, that abuse is not behavior that makes us uncomfortable; it is behavior designed to limit our ability to respond honestly and openly for fear of reprisal. So your mate can yell, even if you hate it. But your mate cannot yell to make you keep quiet, to intimidate you, to force you to behave in a certain way. We are allowed to make each other uncomfortable, but we are not allowed to try to control each other by words, threatened or actual violence, or humiliation.

I was concerned about abuse between the Castigliones. Jody's verbal barrage was clearly limiting Brian's ability to speak for himself. She was humiliating him, and she cut him off when he did try to speak. He had taken the path of least resistance; he allowed her to keep him from talking for himself. They needed to set some new rules for interaction to protect Brian's rights and to force him to participate in his marriage.

Re-establishing Brian's right—and responsibility—to talk for himself required that Jody listen to him even when he disagreed with her. This is a gradual process, one that must be tested by time. Brian and Jody had to experiment with new ways of communicating, ones that at first seemed gimmicky and uncomfortable. Because there was so much anger between them,

I decided against giving them a clear communication task, such as Exercise 5 (Chapter 2). I was afraid that it would be too difficult for them to succeed. Instead, I instructed them in the following exercise.

> EXERCISE 35: For one week, read to each other at night before bedtime. Alternate reader and listener, and read for at least twenty minutes. You may have to negotiate the book to be read, but be sure that it holds interest for the listener. I think it best that the reading be done in bed, just as if you were a small child.

Couples often enjoy this task, as it is relaxing and reminiscent of comforting childhood memories. The Castigliones, though, were uncomfortable with the exercise and spent much time arguing about the rules. Did Brian get to pick a book that Jody would hate? (No.) Could they keep the TV on? (No.) What if the phone rang? (Ignore it and return the call later.) Did they have to read the same book to each other, or could they read different books? (Different books is fine.) When they returned the following week, I was curious about whether they had found a way to sabotage the task. Happily, they had not, and had even improved my assignment.

Brian started. "We had a lot of trouble agreeing on a book. I only read manuals at work, so I thought it would be boring to read just to make Jody happy. And she hates to read. So she said she wouldn't do it." Jody nodded, with a big smile for her husband. "So we talked about what we wanted to read, and what we wanted to know about. Jody found some information about buying a house, how you do it. So we read that for two nights. Then we read some stuff about decorating on a budget. And both of us liked reading that. What should we do next?"

I was thrilled. This argumentative couple had already made major strides. Not only was Brian talking, but the Castigliones had found topics they were both interested in, subjects that were hopeful and forward-looking. They had made changes in their interactions and they were planning for their future!

This was a good sign. Brian and Jody had taken the task assigned them and had improved it. They had talked about what they didn't like about their homework, then adapted the assignment to meet their needs. When people expand an exercise, such as the ones in this book, they are revising it to make it more personal. They are taking ownership of their learning and growth—behavior that always accelerates change.

What else had changed? The Castigliones were sitting closer to each other, Brian spoke; Jody smiled. They had attached to each other again. They didn't think that a major transformation had taken place, and it hadn't. All that had happened was that they were working as a couple on the simple task I had given them, so they were able to remember what working as a couple felt like.

Patience

Brian and Jody learned a lesson that all couples need to know. They learned that both partners need to work together toward common goals. They remembered that they were co-workers, not enemies. They realized that there is a win-win solution, but only when both participate in finding that solution. We spent the session focused on the substance of their reading. We spoke about house hunting and decorating. And then we talked about what they had done so well in the previous week—and how they could continue it. Brian said it best. "When we act as if we're a couple, then we feel like a couple." He beamed at Jody.

The lessons the Castigliones learned were not complicated. Their relief was quick. They were able to make changes in their relationship, to gradually become more trusting and relaxed. That ability to relax in intimate relationships is essential. All too often, we evaluate our marriages as though the relationship of today will never change. As soon as the Castigliones had a joint task to perform, their therapy homework, they were able to pull together and work as a couple. They demonstrated that they could still do what it takes; that they could change.

What they needed to develop was patience. They had to understand that their relationship was a long-term proposition, that the marriage of today could be changed to a different marriage tomorrow. The Castigliones were negotiating how they would remake their marriage, a negotiation essential to all marriages.

The rules for change are often as important as the actual change that eventually takes place in a relationship. Learning how to establish the rules and learning how to permit change are essential in every growing relationship.

Obviously, all relationships change, but few as dramatically as that of parent and child. Parents revel in their children's growth, telling story after story about developmental milestones. We know that the relationship between parent and child must change as the child grows and the parent ages.

EXERCISE 36: Reflect on your relationship with your parents. Of course the relationship has changed as you have grown. How are your interactions different now from what they were when you were a child? How have you and your parents changed the pattern? What do you talk about? What do you do together? How have you established your adulthood with them? How have they accepted—or rejected—your growing independence?

In truth, the development of the parent–child relationship is a wonderful model for change in all our personal interactions. Our human ties must have room for adaptation. We must expect our intimate interactions to evolve with changing situations and advancing time. The issue is not whether we will change, but how we will change, and whether we will permit change in others.

Will we change gracefully? Or kicking and screaming? The Castigliones quickly demonstrated their willingness to strengthen their relationship through change. Their hostility and screaming matches had become transformed into hand-holding. Of course, the work was not completed, but it had begun. Their renewed belief in their ability to change gave them patience, optimism, and hope—it gave them their future back.

Marriage and Growth

Relationships are, at their best, a forum for growth. We learn about ourselves and each other through our intimate interactions. Here, we develop skills in communication, sexuality, and compromise. We experiment with different ways of being. We learn the limitations of anger and the best ways to negotiate. We learn these skills in all our relationships—from parents, siblings, friends, and co-workers. We learn from our enemies. Then we take what we have learned, good and bad, and apply it to our marriages.

The process yields a hodgepodge of ideas about relationships, ideas that must be sorted through within the context of each marriage. Skills of compromise and communication are refined as each couple develops its own set of rules and patterns of negotiation.

One of the most difficult areas to negotiate is compromise. Most of us believe that a reasonable resolution is one that makes both people happy. This is misleading; compromise doesn't make people happy. Basic to the concept of compromise is the acknowledgment that both people have to give. In fact, a reasonable compromise makes both people unhappy—equally unhappy.

This idea surprises many people. We have been trained to

think that a good compromise pleases the participants, even though the very idea of compromise is that we have to give up some of what we really want. People often reject reasonable compromises because the agreement doesn't make them feel good. Indeed, a good compromise makes us tolerably *unhappy.* No person loses significantly more than the other, but *both people lose.* So both are unhappy.

This outcome is not satisfying for many of us, because we believe that marriage should make us happy. We hold on to this wish despite our intellectual understanding that it is wrong. No relationship can make us deliriously happy all the time. People are occasionally disappointing, unable to give what they should. This holds true within marriage; no matter how hard we try and how good our intentions, we inevitably let each other down, time and again.

Marriage, then, must have room for each of us to be dissatisfied and unhappy. We need to understand that our mate will fail us at times, that our spouse cannot meet all our needs. The marriage that lasts is one that survives disappointments and losses. Of course our partners cannot understand all our problems or care about all the things that concern us. But we can develop ways to be different without undermining our intimate connection.

Marriage may not be the solution to all our problems, but it can and should be a safe haven. It can be a place of caring and growth. Over the course of a long marriage, each of us will change a great deal. We may get more politically conservative, gain or lose weight, have a religious awakening. We will respond to normal life-cycle events, such as the death of parents and the birth of children. We may lose an important job or become bored by a dead-end one. We may become ill or disabled. The partners must adapt to such changes through growth.

How does growth happen? It takes place naturally, as long as we do not rigidly stand in its way. We all change and develop through our life experiences. When couples share these experiences or talk about their reactions, they are more likely to grow toward each other, even when the issue is difficult. In fact, we grow through stress and its aftermath.

Why Be Married?

Why should we be married? Why should we endure relationships that are not always good, not always satisfying? Why should we stay with a partner who makes us unhappy some of the time, frustrated at others? Why should we compromise our needs and wants? People in happy marriages recognize that the relationship is a net plus, that what we give has an indirect return. Most spouses realize both people will be happier, over the long haul, if each gives a little for the greater good. We must take care not only of each other, but of the marital bond as well. So when we say "marriage takes work," what we really mean is "marriage takes attention."

Attention? As opposed to work? This attention is an awareness of the other person and of the essential differences and similarities that exist between any pair of individuals. It is attention to that person's needs and feelings, even when they are in conflict with our own. It is a willingness to adapt with—not against—your mate. It is understanding that sometimes the relationship has to be more important than either of the partners if it is to survive.

When I sit with a couple in my office, I am always aware of being in the presence not only of two people, but of their relationship as well. This relationship, this unspoken contract, has implicit and explicit rules. It is regulated by give-and-take, an understanding of what each partner can and must do for the other. It is directed by each spouse's belief in the relationship. Keeping a relationship alive and healthy will always require small compromises and, occasionally, big sacrifices. We may need to move away from family, take a new job, or have another child.

We may need to take actions that are difficult and painful—because the relationship requires these offerings. They are part of the emotional contract we call marriage. Ideally, the issue is not *whether* we make these adjustments, but *how* we make these adjustments.

Marriage Is Not Perfect

Adjusting to the imperfections of the marital bond is one of the most essential—and most difficult—tasks of early marriage. We all hope that we have found a true soulmate, a partner who will not disappoint us. In fact, none of us ever finds the perfect mate. Early marriage is, in part, a period of adjustment to the failings of our chosen partner. The ability to look beyond this person's imperfections to her or his important attributes may well be what keeps marriage from becoming divorce. We each must find ways to accept the person we have married. It is imperative that we find contentment within the bounds of our own marriage, rather than looking around for what we are not getting.

Finding contentment is not easy. It is a long process, one that has to take place over and over again during marriage and is, in fact, a good long-term objective. It is a feeling that we're at home, safe, understood. It is being comfortable with your mate, even when you're angry or embarrassed or ashamed. It is the knowledge that your relationship can tolerate stress and disappointment, can create good from bad. It is, in some sense, the ultimate success.

Many couples are surprised at the stress involved in a wedding. We fight, we cry, we make up. We are shocked at the intensity of our feelings, and at the decibel level of the quarrels. Amazingly, most couples come through the rough period of engagement and wedding not only intact, but strengthened in their commitment. We find ways to split up the work and to bargain for what we want. How we do this may predict how we will negotiate future high-stress issues: where we live, when we have children or buy a house, whose family hosts us for holidays.

The stress of a wedding is a wonderful opportunity for a young couple to begin—or to continue—the process of working toward a common goal. It is a time to put in place many of the skills they will need to make their marriage as good as it can be. Marriage is not the cure for all that ails us, but it is a wonderful and exciting journey in uncharted waters. It can— and should—be a lot of fun!

SUGGESTIONS FOR FURTHER THOUGHT

- How has your marriage changed since your wedding? What hopes did you have then? How do they differ from your hopes now?

- What have you learned about your partner since your wedding? About yourself? How has this knowledge changed or strengthened your marriage?

- What would you want to do to commemorate your commitment to your spouse? What does your partner want to do? Enjoy these things, together.